MW01248649

The Aftermath of
Brown v.
Board of
Education

CHARLES L. MOORE CPA

Copyright © 2021 Charles L. Moore CPA
All rights reserved
First Edition

PAGE PUBLISHING, INC.
Conneaut Lake, PA

First originally published by Page Publishing 2021

ISBN 978-1-6624-3145-6 (pbk)
ISBN 978-1-6624-3146-3 (digital)

Printed in the United States of America

CONTENTS

FOREWORD

THE RECENT PRESIDENTIAL election produced a new democratic party president, Joseph Biden, and the first female, Black and Asian vice president, Kamala Harris. Also, Democrats will continue to control the US House of Representatives and the US Senate. Also, prior to the recent elections, President Donald Trump had just appointed Justice Amy Coney Barrett to replace the late liberal Justice Ruth Bader Ginsburg, thereby tipping the balance in the US Supreme Court toward conservatives. America's polity will likely continue to be polarized for at least two decades, creating some uncertainties about the standing and survival of key polities that are highly controversial, including the status of Brown versus Board of Education of Topeka. The likelihood of a US Supreme Court review of Brown versus Board of Education within the next decade ranges from very high to almost certain.

The policy direction set forth by the landmark ruling, Brown versus Board of Education, was a tipping point in the status of minorities in America. Brown versus Board of Education lies at the nexus between American conscience, politics, decency, aspirations, ethnicity, power, and justice. It is a prime focal point for those who see minority education as central to their search for the nation's soul.

For some, especially members of minority groups, Brown versus Board of Education is at the heart of the pursuit of equity and the socioeconomic transformation of people of color, most of whom live

5

in America's urban areas. For other groups, it is a policy that has gone too far and now represents an instrument of excessive political correctness. As with most other wicked problems, opinions have been formed around both sides of the divide based on limited information and knowledge about what Brown versus Board of Education actually stands for.

If there is ever a time when the nation needs a comprehensive evaluation of Brown versus Board of Education, it is now. *The Aftermath of Brown Versus Board of Education* by Charles L. Moore delivers this knowledge, packed appropriately with the historical and emotional recollection it deserves and the future promise it offers. What is most unique about this book is its full discourse of the social, political, economic, historical, cultural, and power politics underpinnings, the adoption process, the etiology of its management, and consequences of Brown versus Board of Education, one of America's landmark rulings.

By going way back over 200 years to the period of slavery in America, Charles L. Moore demonstrates that Brown versus Board of Education has its roots in the conflicting interests of slaves and slave masters during the darkest period of American history. He showed that education was the only pathway to economic advancement for slaves, although it was largely an unexercisable option. Charles also makes the case that most people of color yearned for education while their slave masters and others abhorred the idea of providing access to slaves. This situation persisted for almost two centuries. A series of landmark legislations eventually paved the way for Brown versus Board of Education: (1) the Thirteenth Amendment to the US Constitution by the US Senate in January of 1865, which abolished slavery; (2) the Fourteenth Amendment in 1868, which granted citizenship to all persons born or naturalized in the United States; and (3) the Fifteenth Amendment, which granted the right to vote. But people of color realized that the ultimate liberalization required equal access to education.

Funding is critical to operationalizing the education pathway to prosperity for people of color. Hence, the quest for educational equity remained a goal of people of color for almost one hundred years after the emancipation amendments above. Brown versus Board of Education became the essential instrument that paved the way for more equitable educational access and prosperity when the case was adjudicated in 1954. But Charles Moore makes the case real by building his introductory chapter around his mother, Pearlie Williams, and Pearlie's parents, an evangelist and a domestic worker in Marion Alabama. Back then, in most of Alabama, you either worked as a field worker on White-owned farms or as a domestic worker serving White families to keep food on the table. And if you are certifiably docile and sufficiently nonbelligerent, you may be trusted enough with the spiritual calming of other Blacks as an evangelist. Pearlie's parents earned their living this way to support their family of ten. Educating as many of their kids was the primary way to bring their large family out of poverty.

Cities like Philadelphia, Detroit, and Baltimore were probably unimaginable to Pearlie's parents as the places where major future battles for education will eventually take place. But today, these places are at the center of the national debate about how to fund their schools equitable. When Brown versus Board of Education affirmed equitable funding for schools in 1954, it was probably the boldest act of emancipation in the history of America. Since then, it served an important purpose and continues so in many parts of the country. But like anything else that tugs at the heart and conscience of America, the work is never done, as power, money, and politics will be sure to motivate challenges to real advancement.

Charles Moore hits on the central issue at the heart of America today: the efficacy and impacts of Brown versus Board of Education. In this book, Charles Moore explained how the politics of urban education is being shaped by changing demographics, White flight from Black urban neighborhoods, and then the flight of an elite class of Black middle class from many cities. Today, while funding for education remains based on the tenets of Brown versus Board of Education, Charles Moore challenges its current and recent administration and its educational outcomes and accomplishments. With so many illiterate school-age children in many of our school systems today, Charles Moore calls for a new paradigm in school funding and administration. The alternatives he offers involve a more comprehensive set of policy instruments, as the police reform, prison system reform, residency requirements for administrators and teachers, curricula shift, and new regulatory reforms must all be part of the solution set. He also discusses a series of intricate aspects such as school funding, educational effectiveness, budgetary responsibilities, assessments, teacher qualification, parents' roles, teachers' roles, and unions. His pay-for-performance model may well be an excellent paradigm for future education funding.

In summary, *The Aftermath of Brown Versus Board of Education* by Charles L. Moore is a must-read for teachers, school administrators, township officials, and policymakers who are serious about an honest debate about America's premier educational policy instrument aimed at access to K–12 education.

Soji Adelaja, PhD
John A. Hannah Distinguished Professor
Michigan State University

CHAPTER ONE

Before Brown v. Board of Education

I ENVISION MY mother, Pearlie Williams, a beautiful, young, and vibrant Black woman, walking down a dirt road in rural Marion, Alabama. The shabby, small Black schools in this town lacked transportation for their students, and the children often had to walk great distances to get to school. My mother was the daughter of an evangelist and a domestic worker. She had four brothers and three sisters—a unique family, because with eight children, each sister had a brother near her age to protect her, if needed.

My mother and her siblings attended a segregated school for Black children in the middle of a rural Alabama town. The school building was barely heated and poorly ventilated. It had a small wood-burning stove and a leaky roof. The children that attended were clearly there to learn, primarily by choice. If discipline was needed, their parents would support it. The parents knew that this school was the only way for their children to have a chance at a better life than their parents and grandparents had.

In the Black community, education was strongly encouraged. An education meant equal opportunities for a better life, which was a dream Blacks collectively shared. As a way to strengthen control over Negroes during the era of slavery, they were prohibited from learning to read and write. Learning to read often yielded severe punishment, including maiming or death. Slave owners, of whom many were uneducated themselves, knew that if slaves could read and write, they had a better chance of escaping unjust bondage and systematic dehumanization. Escaped slaves could take hold of their rightful share of the great American pie.

There has always been confusion as to why the practice of prohibiting slaves from reading was necessary to maintain control over them. One theory is that not being able to read kept slaves tied to the plantation where they lived and worked. Slaves' work was back-breaking labor, under abysmal conditions. In most cases, the number of slaves outnumbered the number of owners and caretakers. One might believe that an escape could be possible. However, the question would always be "Who will lead the group to freedom?"

Another important question remained unanswered: "Where is freedom?" If you cannot read or write, would you know how to get to freedom? When you got there, wherever "there" happened to be, how would you know that you had arrived?

Then there was the notion that following the North Star would lead you to freedom. But how would you follow the North Star during the day and during cloudy nights when there are no stars in the sky? You had to be able to read.

Is there any difference between the era of slavery and the present time? Today, the inability to read still exists, predominately among Black citizens. If you cannot read, how do you travel to your aunt's house in Ohio? How do you find a job or complete a job application?

White America was reluctant and went to great extremes to avoid sharing America's wealth and riches with anyone of color. Blacks were earmarked to hold the lowest-ranking job, and the situation still exists today. There are generations of Black individuals that continue to be trapped by their circumstances. Although there are no current White slave masters limiting Black children's opportunity to learn, it is sad to say that most urban schools are now administratively led by African American board members that have the power to provide unlimited educational opportunities for Black children. School administration personnel in urban areas are predominately African American, but African American representation in teacher ranks has declined. The question is, Are the current slave masters BLACK? Is there such a thing?

White control limited educational opportunities, and the lack of equal funding became the next roadblock. Now that Black and Brown people are firmly in control of most urban school districts, funding has somewhat equalized. The problem now is that many Black students continue to be plagued by poor academic achievement, despite the fact that many school board members, superintendents, principals, and school program department heads are Black or Brown.

In lower socioeconomic communities, social welfare programs are not requiring mothers—and sometimes fathers—to work, giving parents the time to work with students to improve their academic performance. Could it be that the Black leadership structure is also racist? Can Blacks be racist against other Blacks? Or is the real dividing line not race, but economic and social status?

Brown v. Board of Education of Topeka provided the pathway to equal funding for students. Could equal opportunity for funding actually have become the beginning of the end? Or could it have triggered the great intellectual brain drain from urban neighborhoods?

Amid the great struggle for equality, the intellectual African American white-collar working class and well-paid union workforce began taking full advantage of equal funding and integration to move their families out of Black neighborhoods. This left the blue-collar nonunion working class to deal with criminal elements that became dominant in urban neighborhoods.

As African Americans started to leave urban areas, police forces began limiting or eliminating the requirement that peace officers live in the communities they serve. When Black intellectuals and unionized workers left for the suburbs, their ways of living and priorities transferred to their new locations. This brought on a new set of challenges. Assimilating into traditional White suburbs left little time to address the continued struggles in the urban areas.

As most of the suburban Blacks were of the African American leadership class, there came a shift in the civil rights struggle. Peace officers traditionally kept the peace because their families and friends lived in the neighborhoods they served, and they wanted to lessen the chances of criminal activities there. When peace officers transitioned into patrol officers, because their families and friends no longer lived in the communities they served, they lost touch with the actions of their own communities and also lost touch and relationships with the criminal elements of the urban neighborhoods.

With peace officers' loss of connectivity to urban neighborhoods, the neighborhoods lost control of crime. As crime increased, the more mobile, educated, and unionized members of the Black workforce moved to the suburbs, looking for greater opportunities. Their family's increased crime in the old neighborhoods blocked them from returning once they discovered that "the grass isn't always greener on the other side."

The teachers and administrators followed, and the deterioration of the urban schools increased more rapidly. As the great migration continued, the more highly educated affluent Blacks moved out of the neighborhoods, but they become leaders of the schools in the neighborhoods they left.

Upon moving their families out of the Black neighborhoods into the White suburbs and returning to take on higher-level administrative positions within the Black schools, this group of educators ignited one of the greatest debates of Black progress: The debate between W. E. B. Du Bois's and Booker T. Washington's visions for urban education. These two Black men were great leaders of the Black community, holding significant places in African American history. However, each had a distinctly different vision for his community. They successfully enjoyed their share of the American dream, which only a good education and/or business ownership could provide.

Leadership was achieved by individuals with formal educations nearly 100% of the time. Leaders included members of boards of education, superintendents, principals, and department heads. They were almost exclusively college-educated, suburban Blacks that lacked any similarities to the students they were to educate, except for the Black skin they shared. Other current life experiences almost never intersected. So then, what's the difference between those Black leaders and White leaders? When you get that level of concentration of educated and uneducated Blacks, you start to get efforts to replicate their college success in others and almost eliminate other avenues for success, such as middle school athletics, performing arts, and industrial arts.

Du Bois had the primary idea that Blacks needed to take advantage of the middle-class lifestyle by becoming better educated and competing for jobs that Whites dominated. He felt that Blacks should strive to become educated in colleges and universities in greater numbers. He believed that manual labor was a thing of the past and held no promise for Blacks. As the educated suburban Blacks became dominant in Black education, it was time to move the Blacks to a more highly educated group and leave manual labor jobs behind, whether they led to good-paying jobs or not. This thought was without any consideration for the fact that most Black business successes are in labor-related fields, in which there has been a legacy since coming over from Africa on slave ships.

On the other hand, Booker T. Washington had been successful in integrating vocational education into urban communities where less than 25% of Blacks were college bound. The fields of study the students were engaged in were concentrated in just a few areas. Washington believed that business and skilled trades were at the forefront of Blacks' economic prominence a few years before Brown v. Board of Education was enacted.

The Du Bois theory became a prominent way of thinking. Those in leadership began to increase college-bound opportunities and, for the most part, to eliminate Washington's programs in general. The vocational education programs were dismantled by Black-controlled leadership, leaving non-college-bound students limited opportunities, which led to decreased job opportunities.

To compound the problem, the students receiving the attention were college bound. School boards, with their concentration of college-educated and suburban administrations, began eliminating most other opportunities for urban students that were not college bound. They started making it harder for students that did not want to go to college to stay in school at all. Because of high-stakes testing, poor-performing students hurt the schools' overall performance, dragging the districts' performance into the ground. So, they concentrate on college-bound students instead. The college-bound students primarily used this opportunity as a way to get out of the neighborhood, leaving non-college-bound students with fewer opportunities to earn a decent living wage. This, in turn, drove them in increasing numbers to criminal activity.

The community suffered as the intellectuals took advantage of the newfound opportunities. They headed to the suburbs to spend their money, raise their children, and add to the talent pool in the suburban communities. Oddly enough, despite their accomplishments, they remained outsiders in those communities. They may have been able to secure the house and white picket fence, but definitely were not included in the backyard across-the-fence conversations of their White neighbors. They were simply tolerated, not celebrated or encouraged to bring their friends.

As White America identified the divide in the Black communities, it forced Blacks to label other Blacks as special needs or at-risk, which only increased the tension between these two groups of Blacks. With the introduction of standards testing, which middle-class and affluent Blacks' children did well on compared to urban youth, educated Blacks now had power over non-college-bound Black students like slave masters once did. Because Black-on-Black crime is tolerated, the educated Blacks even took the opinion that since White-on-White crime is at the same rate statistically, Black-on-Black crime is at a tolerable level and doesn't need to be discussed. So, the parents of Black individuals that are killed by White perpetrators, which receive international support, are left to suffer the loss in silence. This situation increased the divide between the more affluent and unionized Blacks and urban neighborhood Blacks. No one even took a second look at the academic injustices being committed against these urban students.

But White America had the solution. Charter schools were an alternative for Black families to escape the Black oppressor. So today, almost three million students have left their Black oppressor school systems for the mostly White administratively dominated charter school system. Introducing the charter school system resulted in school district funding cuts, which caused Black leadership to double down on college education, their comfort zone, and increased the pressure of high-stakes testing. This continued to separate the two Black groups. Divide and conquer! That is the American way.

During the period of slavery, slaves could only dream of such a life. In the midst of their captivity, they would always dream of a better life. Once the shackles were broken and the door of escape crept open, education was the map needed to navigate unchartered territories. Now that former slaves were free in America, their education was absolutely necessary to avoid other barriers and pitfalls caused by being illiterate. Can you imagine living in a land and never being able to understand what people were communicating through the written word? Or can you imagine not being able to leave your familiar surroundings because you could not follow signs or able to travel to unknown territories?

One of the statistics people do not fully comprehend is how many people are not able to read. Take public transportation for example. Most of the instructions are not just in the written word. They are depicted in symbols and various colors to accommodate people that cannot read. The person speaking over the public address system in the bus or at the transit system bus stop announces that you are on the YELLOW line and this is the stop. This is so that people that lack the ability to read know where to get off the bus.

In America, one of the richest countries in the world, there is still a large population of individuals that cannot read. During biblical times, lepers had lesions on their bodies and were thrown together into colonies to live and suffer and eventually die. Today, illiteracy is treated the same way leprosy was during biblical times, but now the colonies where illiterate people are thrown together are jail or prison. Approximately 70% of prison inmates are functionally illiterate. We find that the common denominator among prisoners weighs heavier on literacy than on race.

During the period of slavery in America, slaves compensated for not being able to read or write by using their natural instincts. In the woods, they would follow the paths of rivers and inspect plants and moss growing on trees, which indicated the northerly direction.

Stars in the night sky served as their global positioning system (GPS). Slaves created code songs such as "Follow the Drinking Gourd" to relay directions to other slaves. Once they had exhausted those resources, traveling or communicating with others was difficult. Slaves dreamed and prayed that future generations of their descendants would be able to read and write. Reading and writing not only enhanced physical freedom but also allowed the mind to travel as far as it could imagine. It sparked creativity and increased the ability to destroy debilitating barriers.

Once slaves were able to read and write, one cannot help but take notice of how many Black inventors surfaced. Simple inventions existed even during slavery; but once the Black man and woman engaged in mathematics, science, physics, and other educational disciplines, they began to change the world with their inventions in ever-increasing numbers. Blacks were determined to overcome the limitations forced upon their ancestors.

The million-dollar question is, if you are able to read, is college the only route to financial success? Is entrepreneurial and skilled labor also a pathway for financial success? Can we afford to leave those disciplines to the remainder of Americans? My opinion is a flat NO.

My mother Pearlie had to walk three miles per day on hot and dusty roads to and from the little school building. She grew accustomed to it, and most days were not that bad, because the goal of becoming educated was at the forefront of her mind and in everyone else's in the Black community.

During Pearlie's high school years, there was a young man who fancied her. His name was Charles L. Moore. My mother always talked about how handsome a man and what a gentleman he was. He made sure her travels to and from school were safe and without incident. Ms. Pearlie Mae Williams was a spry young lady who took education very seriously. She excelled in English and was known for her ability to write. She was kind enough to assist some of the other students with their homework and grammar lessons. Pearlie's proficiency in this area led to her being crowned Spelling Bee Champion.

Envision that at that time, there was limited school busing for Black students. The schools were poorly funded. Teachers were paid wages that were far lower than what their counterparts at White majority schools earned. The teachers and staff were paid menial salaries, but the community members willingly subsidized their living expenses in appreciation of their sacrifices for the betterment of the race.

Residents of the community placed teachers at a high level of regard. Teachers made themselves available in the evening if the day's homework was a little harder than normal and they were not able to successfully get the point across during the day. The Black community appreciated teachers and would provide important items needed to enhance their standard of living, items they couldn't afford on a teacher's salary. Everyone knew that good teachers were needed to improve the education of the race and necessary to make up for the many years Blacks were not allowed the opportunity to learn.

Fast-forward to 2020. Very few teachers live in the neighborhoods where they teach. In fact, urban school systems are poorly funded—not with financial resources, but with parental support in the community. Can you image a parent going into a parent-teacher conference or meeting with someone at the school and having to reveal that they cannot read themselves? So, what most parents do is not attend at all. If you reveal your inability to read to someone, the news is probably not going to spread through the neighborhood. But if you discuss it with one of the Black leadership team members, it may get back to your friends or associates. So, what do you do? You just do not come to meet the teacher.

The predominately working-class Blacks fantasized about how their lives could be changed if they were given a chance at obtaining a formal education. Without that chance, they would be limited to backbreaking labor, which in rural America was the fate of most Black men and women. Racism kept their names off the "good jobs" list. With the hope of securing a job with pay sufficient enough to provide for their families, Blacks knew that they had to know twice as much and work three times as hard as Whites. They had to get all of the education possible to even compete with the uneducated Whites vying for the same positions. Can you imagine the constant fear of being beaten and whipped if you were caught reading a book? Black people had to hide and take that chance in order to learn what should have been their God-given right.

Now, let's take a look at the year 2020, where elementary and secondary education is free and mandatory. Illiteracy and truancy rates are over 65% and 35%, respectively, among Blacks. Schools are generally funded as White communities, but Blacks control educational opportunities. Are we better off? The dreams of our forefathers are dying. The opportunity for Black children to have education available for them to read and write adequately and be able to operate in the United States with access to the "American dream" is disappearing.

Blacks have control of the budget and hold top educational positions in most major cities with a Black majority. So, why are our children not being educated? Is it that suburban Black educators are not holding up their end of the bargain after the landmark ruling in Brown v. Board of Education? It is my opinion that our own Black educators have left the Black communities in the urban areas and blame failure on the poor Black parents that lack the education and resources to help their families. Educators condemn students for not wanting to be college-educated by eliminating every avenue to success except the college route. Black educators are killing students' dreams of escaping street gangs or hate groups. There is no one holding educators accountable for their actions of miseducating the urban Black and poor youth in America.

In 1896, the U.S. Supreme Court issued a landmark decision known as Plessy v. Ferguson. After the Reconstruction era, the freedmen were free, but they were unable to enjoy their freedom. The Thirteenth, Fourteenth, and Fifteenth Amendments to the U.S. Constitution were not sufficient to equalize the races. The Thirteenth Amendment "abolished slavery and involuntary servitude, except as punishment for a crime." This amendment was passed by the Senate on April 8, 1864, and by the House of Representatives on January 31, 1865.

In 1868, the Fourteenth Amendment was ratified to the U.S. Constitution. This amendment granted citizenship to all persons born or naturalized in the United States—including former slaves—and guaranteed all citizens equal protection of the laws. Further, the Fourteenth Amendment states, "No State shall make or enforce any law which shall abridge the privileges or immunities of citizens of the United States; nor shall any state deprive any person of life, liberty, or property, without due process of law; nor deny to any person within its jurisdiction the equal protection of the laws." As you can already imagine, these amendments met opposition and resistance from various groups of people.

It was not until the Fifteenth Amendment was ratified that African Americans finally, with reluctance, were given the right to vote. This amendment states that "the rights of citizens of the United States to vote shall not be denied or abridged by the United States or by any state on account of race, color, or previous condition of servitude."

In Louisiana, a social reform group of prominent Black, Creole, and White New Orleans residents formed the Citizens' Committee. They wanted to repeal or challenge the law that required Blacks to ride in railcars separate from Whites. This group chose a man named Homer Plessy, who was seven-eighths White and one-eighth Black and could pass for White. Homer purchased a ticket and sat in the White section of the railcar. When asked to move to the "colored" car because someone believed he was Black, he refused to move and was, of course, arrested. Although seven of his ancestors were White and one was Black, he was refused the right to sit in a train car, because he was considered Black. This case resulted in the enactment of racial segregation laws, nicknamed "Jim Crow" laws. The state ruled that equality referred to "absolute equality under the law and not social equality under the law." In a nutshell, it said that as long as the facilities were equal in quality it was legal to separate the races. This ruling grew to become known as the doctrine of "separate but equal."

One only needs to take a look at water fountains, restrooms, and other facilities to realize that "separate but equal" could not have been further from the truth. A series of these "Jim Crow" laws were instituted and spread like wildfire across the southern states, and Jim Crow practices spread northward soon thereafter. In essence, Jim Crow made it possible for states to legalize racial segregation in hotels, restaurants, and beaches. Education was no different.

Despite the push for quality education in the Black community, there were still some young men that preferred to play eight ball rather than spend time learning how to read and write. The principal of my mother's school would stop by local pool halls frequently, if not daily, checking to see if his students were hanging out there, instead of being in school. The only people hanging out at such places were wayward individuals that were content to work small labor jobs or enjoy libations. They were content with drinking liquor as opposed to learning to read and write. There were certainly enough menial labor jobs in the fields and local factories that would allow people to eke out a meager living and maintain such lifestyles. However, there was nothing desirable about this lifestyle. The Black community, descendants of slaves, knew that educating themselves was the only way to bring about a more prosperous lifestyle, thus the push for quality education.

For so long, Jim Crow laws, resulting from Plessy v. Ferguson, touted the so-called virtues of "separate but equal" and prohibited young Blacks from obtaining adequate, let alone equal, education. Black schools and their buses, equipment, books, and supplies were supposed to be equal to that of their White counterparts. Nothing could have been further from the truth. My mother and others endured the leaky ceilings, the smell of wood-burning stoves, and walking miles to and from school. They believed that adequate education was the ticket to getting better jobs, rather than having to endure the menial jobs reserved for the uneducated Negro. Menial jobs helped to feed and provide for the family; however, the income from those jobs was only slightly higher than the income earned from sharecropping.

Plessy v. Ferguson did not solve the problems for Blacks. Yes, supposedly Blacks were allowed to have "equal" access to the same tools, but history proves otherwise. It was not until 1954 that another landmark case, Brown v. Board of Education of Topeka, dealt a deadly blow to Plessy v. Ferguson.

Let's discuss the fact that even after the implementation of Brown v. Board of Education, many schools remained virtually segregated because of neighborhood patterns. In the 1970s, some school districts sought to integrate, and some were forced by courts to achieve a racial balance using tactics such as busing students to schools outside their neighborhoods. However, in 2007, a divided Supreme Court ruled that public schools "cannot seek to achieve or maintain integration through measures that take explicit account of a student's race."

In January 2012, *The New York Times* reported on a study by the Manhattan Institute that found segregation in US neighborhoods had greatly declined and that "the nation's cities are more racially integrated than at any time since 1910." While, as the article noted, the findings were generally accepted by a number of experts, some argued that the decline in busing to achieve racial integration resulted in more racially segregated public schools in some areas than before.

What are your thoughts on the evolution of racial integration of public schools in the United States since Brown versus Board of Education? The crafter of the litigation could not in his wildest imagination believe that an estimated 80% of direct educators would not be residents of the communities they serve. A little discussed provision of Brown v. Board of Education was the increase in Black teacher wages along with the wages of their White counterparts. Because of unionization, that portion of the litigation has been accomplished.

CHAPTER TWO

Did Brown v. Board of Education
Fulfill the Dream?

So, was the American educational system finally enjoyed by one big happy family? Nothing could be further from the truth. The Supreme Court probably never imagined the extent people would take to avoid integration. Resistance in Prince Edward County, Virginia, led to school closures from 1959 to 1964. Imagine opposing desegregation to the point of closing down good schools to avoid allowing Blacks to attend along with White children. The wealthy were able to send their children to neighboring schools. The Blacks in that area went from attending poor shabby schools with precious few resources to finally being allowed to go to public schools with the White kids, to having the school doors padlocked and the windows boarded up so that no one could attend.

Some Blacks were able to attend makeshift schools staffed by volunteers from across the country. Those that could afford to had to move in with relatives and attend schools in other parts of the county. Others simply missed out on educational opportunities for five years, often never being able to overcome this misfortune. There are stories of children that weren't allowed to attend school and that were never able to finish school. Some lost interest; some were too engaged in seeking out a living, sometimes working fifteen to sixteen hours a day. Others that had grown to adulthood took the time to attend night school to catch up on several years of missed opportunities.

Imagine the emotional toll on young Black children that knew without a doubt that Whites hated integration to the extent of simply closing and shutting down their own so-called good schools. This was just one display of protest. It took decades for Prince Edward County, Virginia, to desegregate. Out of a roll of 204,000 Black students in September 1960, only 170 were enrolled in White schools. Although our ancestors dreamed of the day that our young people could be afforded the right to equal education, our young people were not able to see it come to fruition. Did they lose hope?

Since Brown v. Board of Education was enacted, several historical events have taken place. One memorable event, The Little Rock Nine, was a pivotable moment of the civil rights movement; history was changed. In 1957, Arkansas Governor Orval Faubus, in defiance of a federal court order, brought in the National Guard to ensure that only White students were allowed to enter Central High School. Nine Black students that were hand-selected by the NAACP for their academic abilities were chosen to integrate Central High School but were refused entry. The President of the United States had to call in the military, paratroopers of the 101st Airborne Division, to escort the nine Black children through the crowd of angry protesters. Even this shameful event did not diminish the widespread systemic inequality that permeated the educational system.

It may appear that most of the data used in this book is relative primarily to Blacks. For the most part, it is. Brown v. Board of Education and Plessy v. Ferguson affected Blacks; therefore, it lends to the fact that this book, *Aftermath of Brown v. Board of Education* would do the same.

I want to explore the myth that schools are separate and funding is equal. Blacks that had money were able to attend public schools in most of the neighborhoods in which they lived. Upward mobility or financial means you could afford continued quality education. We will discuss that most of the students in the 1950s and 1960s had to find a job in order to keep food on the table and help maintain shelter for the family. Most of the available work in rural areas was farming-related and, in the more urban areas, construction. Parents needed their children's assistance in other trade jobs to ensure that enough funds were coming into the household to maintain a stable home. Usually, the employers were family- or White-owned businesses. Is the same thing happening now? It is an interesting concept that young people did not attend school because of family financial worries.

With the creation of public assistance, the basic needs of food and shelter are covered. Why then is student attention still a major issue? If children are not going to school, what is keeping them from attending school on a regular basis if covering the family's basic survival needs is not the reason?

There are factors that have overridden this issue. The first is that in single-parent households, one of the requirements for public housing is that the father of the children cannot be in the home. Also, course offerings in urban schools have been limited to classes that allow students to pass a proficiency test on which all schools are graded. Trade and life skills courses have been discontinued in urban areas so that students can pass a test that is primarily developmental by middle- and upper-class citizens' standards. Schools are testing background knowledge of things that students learn in a middle-class setting. This puts urban children at a disadvantage.

Because life skills are not being taught in schools, urban youth are learning those skills from community individuals that sometimes do not have the best interest of the children in mind. Students are not learning much more than test-taking skills, which are not very useful in the real world. There is not a promise of additional compensation if you test well and do not attend college, but go directly to the workforce. The only change is that they are just working as business owners or employed by criminals or, in some capacity, in the underground economy that exists and flourishes in the urban and rural areas.

Young urban and rural youth have to make a career choice early. If you are not going to college and vocational education has been eliminated, then one of the few lucrative trades that our youth can see operating in full force, each and every day of their lives, is the larger than life, glorified on television and in the movies, life of crime. These criminal elements live in the communities and are readily available. They tend to possess the most beautiful women and cars and have lots of money. Criminals are usually very supportive of the young men in the neighborhood, because the youth provide a ready workforce to exploit as illegal money-making ventures are considered. Seeing this lifestyle glorified by Blacks in the media, our youth are numbed to the inherent dangers and lulled by modern-day Pied Pipers to the pit of prison and early graves, with no hope of escape.

A way out is via the athletic fields of basketball, baseball, football, or track. Other escapes are in disciplines such as dancing, singing, drama, and the arts. Over the years, those opportunities have been eliminated in most urban school districts due to the competition for staff and the continued need for increasing or maintaining the wages of professional staff. Middle school athletics and the arts have been eliminated to maintain wages. Those wages have been squeezed because local, state, and federal revenues have not been able to keep pace with the wage increases, which has led to financial programs being stressed and even eliminated. The priority in urban districts has been on maintaining wages for the professional staff, as opposed to maintaining arts and sports programs for the students. Combined with the elimination of vocational education, the career path for urban and rural poor and lower-middle-class youth is brighter in the business of crime than in going to school. The dropout rate has increased in correlation with the rate of incarceration.

To compound the situation, the W. E. B. Du Bois Black leadership (the Blacks that believe it is college or nothing) have moved their families to nonurban schools where middle school athletics, arts, and vocational education programs are increasing. So, race is not the major factor for urban children; it is economic capacity. Black students in nonurban schools have similar opportunities as White students do, given their zip code. Although there are still roadblocks because of race, there is a distinct difference between suburban and urban Black youth.

This is not to negate the fact that other races have problems in schools, as well. Albeit different, they too have their sets of problems, including automatic weapons, cocaine, heroin and other drugs, mass killings, suicide, hazing, and racist displays; and the list goes on.

The media is quick to point out the problems Black children face in urban school settings. There was a letter written by Christopher Jackson entitled *What It is Like to Teach Black Students*. It was read in a YouTube video and published.[1] The letter was read and recorded by a different person from the one who wrote it. The reader was somewhat trying to justify the information shared in the letter yet was leaving it open for listeners to determine for themselves whether the letter could have actually been written by a professional teacher.

When hearing the person read the letter, one's mind would conjure up images of Black students "acting like crazy and wild animals." The writer and reader both mimic languages supposedly quoted from his Black students. Every sentence was peppered with "damns" and "duh's." All of the students sounded the same. Such language sounded as if it came from one of the 1920s black-and-white reel movies depicting Blacks as mumbling and shuffling illiterates. The writer commented that all of the Blacks were the same. He went on to say that they loved the exact same music, talked exactly alike, used the same gestures, did the same dances, and wore the same clothes. There was no variety except for the various hues of their Black skin. The few Whites at least liked a variety of music—some country, polka, blues, or other genres. They wore different clothes, and each talked in their own unique way.

The writer goes on to say that the letter sounded believable and that it definitely sounded like a real teacher sharing his real-life experiences. As the recording went on, you definitely wondered if the reader and the writer were one and the same. The tone used as he spoke of Blacks was distinctly different from when he referred to the poor unfortunate White students that were subjected to such a circus. He mentioned things such as the majority of Black girls being obese and loving it, often making jokes about their "juicy fruit," seiz-

---

[1]   https://www.youtube.com/watch?v=s1PL3xQu16w

ing every opportunity to gyrate and promenade themselves in front of the sex-crazed boys in the class, whose animalistic instincts left them void of any notions of love and romance. These boys were hard hearted, street talking, vulgar thugs, incapable of understanding love. "Just give me the goods, let me do the do" was their attitude. The way the narrator talked about the raps they spewed out of their mouths and their dancing was embarrassing.

Women in urban areas found themselves in a precarious position. They were no longer required to do the heavy lifting and hard labor, but in exchange, they were bombarded with opportunities that exploited their sexuality. Women were financially and emotionally rewarded for their actions. If a woman was not college material, she quickly realized she could use her sexuality to either partner in a criminal trade or keep having babies, which provided housing and food for the family through social welfare programs. The welfare system provided all of the things a man would normally provide in their lives. If a woman and her children needed food and shelter, her new man was the welfare system. This new system also gave women something that their mother did not have, which is control of the household.

A provision in the welfare and HUD (Section 8) laws prohibit fathers from living in the household. It further reduces benefits if a woman is married to the father of her children or if the father is not on disability. The programs still promote single-parent households.

Black and Brown women then began graduating from college at a rate of seven women to one man. Consequently, the women's income increased, which meant that the financial control of households was being transferred to women in the Black and Brown communities. Can you see the landscape now? Black men were not only under siege by the White communities but also punished for fighting for educational equality. The men that worked hard for educational equality received it somewhat. But it would not be the Black men but rather it would be their women and children that gained the financial reward from the landmark decision.

The end result was the transfer of financial wealth from Black men to Black women. Now, it worked as planned; women were successful in making men's home lives unbearable. Men were no longer in control of their children because of the hostility in the Black household. Divorce rates skyrocketed, which indirectly meant that men lost control of their children due to the lack of their presence. This made men more susceptible to becoming criminal entrepreneurs in Black communities. Now, let's throw in the decline of the Black church. In 1954, 85% of Black families attended church, whereas today, it is less than 25%.

In the Christopher Jackson's story referenced earlier, I know that some of what was said was true: that children need to be "taught" how to act in school, as I have seen myself. However, Mr. Jackson went to great lengths to color the activities and the children as ignorant and proud of being ignorant. According to Mr. Jackson, the Blacks he described said that they regularly declared everything that made sense to normal White people as racist. To the Black students, being asked to study was racist. Doing homework was racist. The writer made it seem like life was one big circus and the Black students were proud to be the entertainment.

If you are White, Asian, or of another race and you watch television, you can clearly see depictions of Blacks in the manner noted in the Jackson story. The majority of Blacks in leadership roles are in schools. Then, how can racism continue? Who would image that Black individuals would not go over and above for students of the same color? Surely, all Blacks know that they share the same struggles!

I was offended by both the reader and the writer. I do not remember any instance in which the teacher mentioned making any efforts to "teach." His "observance" was more as a helpless spectator of the students' shenanigans, not willing to be part of any solution. I would venture to say that his eight-page letter was probably twice as long as his lesson plans for the year. It was more of an "I told you so…let me share the dirt" type of reaction. He took pleasure in simply being a spectator of the chaos as opposed to helping solve the problems. God forbid, teach them anything! What chance does a child have to learn in school if those assigned to teach do not even believe they can be taught or are even worthy of being taught? If the teacher has no expectation of your success, over time, you may not have many expectations for yourself either.

In another YouTube documentary, people talk about the day-to-day life of "at-risk" children living in impoverished neighborhoods. Many of the children attend schools where the breakfast and lunch provided are the only meals they can count on for the day. Coming from single-parent homes, living in poor-quality housing, with many sleeping on pallets on the floor without proper bedding, their living situation did not set the pace for having a good day at school. In colder climates, many children often do not have adequately warm clothing. Imagine children dealing with this type of environment at home and then entering the doors of the schoolhouse greeted by teachers that have no interest in educating them or, worse, do not believe they are capable of learning.

Today, we see that many schools have reverted back to being predominately Black or White. Instead of finding other ways to protest and avoid integration, people have found a way to separate the races. White families put down their picket signs and put up "for sale" signs and moved out to the suburbs to other high-rent neighborhoods, leaving Blacks in their old neighborhoods and old schools.

When you weigh in the fact that school districts are partially supported by property taxes, it is a given that schools in the upscale neighborhoods with expensive homes and higher property taxes definitely have better schools, affording a better education for those children that attend. If that is not enough revenue, they increase fees for student activities because their families can afford it. The nicer schools, of course, attract the best teachers and create an environment for the students to maximize their ability to learn. Again, we see "separate but definitely by no means equal."

Why is it that Black and Brown schools have financial problems, which are primarily due to declining student revenue and increasing labor costs? The unions demand higher wages to teach in urban areas because of the complexities of servicing poor children that lack the essential educational tools that are needed to learn by suburban standards. Higher union wages have afforded the vast majority of the professional staff to live in suburban neighborhoods and then bring those standards to urban neighborhoods. Does standardized testing push their beliefs even further in that direction? Most states have now gone to a school fund method that also takes into account the student population. As academic success declines and crime in schools increases, students look for better education options. Revenue then declines, which in turn affects staff wages. This situation then pushes the better teacher to seek better wages in suburban schools where their own children attend. Why is it that urban school districts with primarily Black and Brown administrative board members with the same unions as in the nonurban areas have affordable contracts, while urban schools have contracts that they cannot afford?

Another practice that separates children within the same schools is called "tracking." Tracking is a subtle way to identify "gifted" children and put them into separate classes. You probably guessed it; these gifted classes have a disproportionate number of White students, and the lion's share of the school's resources are allocated to support them.

Even in majority Black districts, the resources are allocated primarily to the students that are college bound. In most districts, that number is limited to between 15% and 20% of the students. This leaves the remaining 80–85% of the students with classes that are not preparing them for everyday living in the world or for the job market. So, these students are left just hanging in the wind, with diplomas that have little meaning other than showing that the students gained skills on how to take standardized tests. These diplomas have almost zero practical use for everyday living. The children that have the greatest need, again, receive the crumbs, do not have the supplies they need, and have teachers that really do not expect much from them. What is a child to do? They may desire to learn but get the message from those around them that they are not worth the money or the effort.

This is where the rubber meets the road. On the surface, we can compare funding levels, which appear to be equal. Most states provide a per-student payment to each school, based on the actual number of students. Affluent districts usually receive extra funds for extra books, buildings, extracurricular sports activities, and other equipment from student fees. Poor urban districts lack the ability within their communities to raise additional funds. It is a challenge to get property tax increases in school districts where most of the tax-payers' school-aged children do not attend public schools and where professional staff and their children do not attend the public schools in neighborhoods where they work. Therefore, there is limited advocacy for property and other tax increases to better fund the schools.

The actual source of increased income is from federally funded programs for lower-income citizens, based primarily on the number of students that receive free and reduced-cost meals. These students are labeled "at-risk." Funding increases as the districts educate more "at-risk" students. This leads me to the real issue, which is that these funds are for failing schools. Actually, schools that have the worst performance receive more federal assistance. "The money is in failure!"

Let's explore why this is a perfect storm. Students are falling further into peril, and no one seems able to figure out how to teach students to adequately read and write and become productive citizens. We can put people on the moon and develop self-driving automobiles, but we cannot teach poor students how to read and write? Come on now! Or is it really true that there is money in failure?

Unions usually receive 75% of their funding from grants that are earmarked for staffing. They get paid on staff head count, not on performance. So, the more federal support money unions receive, the more dues they can collect. Most of the time, they negotiate contracts with very little accountability for performance. Merit is based primarily on years of satisfactory service, not on student achievement. As the federal government has been implementing more measures of accountability into grants and contracts, the number of teachers and other educational professionals has been in an epidemic decline.

The pressure for student performance is at an all-time high. For unions to continue receiving federal funding, teacher contracts and states are requiring more real-time evaluation of teacher performance, based on academic gains. As these new standards are enacted, the number of teachers is declining at an alarming rate.

Suburban schools have increased efforts to attract staff, but increased performance accountability has not had the same impact there. Who wants to be graded on the academic performance of students that you do not believe can perform? So, the thinking is that it is best to resign before your name is associated with failure and your career is affected. Contracts are usually "one size fits all," and there is little distinction between actual performance. The superintendents, principals, and department heads that are usually disassociated from the students do not live in the district; nor do they usually have school-aged children attending these schools. Their children usually attend suburban schools.

State departments of education, which approve funds spending, have more control over schools' academic programs than the school administrations themselves. School districts with larger numbers of at-risk students have less control, because a larger portion of their schools' budgets come from federal funding. They relinquish substantial control over academic programs in order to obtain approval for grant funds.

The irony is that state departments of education get final approval of academic programs, but are not held accountable and, in most cases, have no proven success at implementing programs that improve outcomes of students living in poverty. If the program that the state department of education approved is unsuccessful, the department takes no responsibility. The staff members are not graded on performance based on the plans they approved. Although boards of education do not have any approval that's required by the state for the schools' improvement plans, they are held accountable for the implementation of those plans. States require boards of education to approve budgets and perform fiscal audits, but not the schools' improvement plans, which should be the primary driver of the budget. Put resources in the areas of financial need.

Federal program grant guidelines may change every six months. However, when people at local levels master the tests or programs, the tests or programs change. Keep in mind that federal funding is primarily through Title I and food services grants. These grants are research in nature, and like any research grant, there is a lot of reporting and paperwork submitted to the granting organization. Ironically, the primary research used by the Bureau of Prisons is from data obtained from grants that are based on a student's ability to read at a third-grade level. In fact, Title I makes the Tuskegee Syphilis Experiment look like child's play. You are talking about control over "at-risk" students all over the United States. You are talking about all control and NO accountability. It is unacceptable what Title I does to the children. It has created the perfect storm for failure with the illusion of improvement.

It is like the biggest game of fantasy football. These people get data, and they analyze the data like fantasy football. This is why not one fantasy football champ has a coaching job in the NFL, because decisions need to be made by a coach with local control that can read the game from a history of success. In this case, not only are they unsuccessful, but also it's getting worse, and yes, what do we do? We pour more money into education. This is why I continue to say that "the money is in failure!"

To summarize, I believe the US Federal Government has analysts that are playing a form of fantasy football with the lives of our students, with NO responsibility or accountability. The states have to implement these federal programs, and they are graded on compliance, not on the success of the program. Additionally, the more failure you have, the more grant funds you can apply for. The unions get higher head counts and additional positions. Lastly, the administration maintains good relationships with the unions assisting them in maintaining staff head counts, although the revenue base is declining. The relationship ensures that staff payroll is the last item to be cut. So, all the extracurricular activities are eliminated to maintain professional staff compensation.

Because the professional staff members do not live in the communities they serve, the lack of extracurricular activities and program elimination has no direct effect on their livelihood or families. Conversely, in the districts where the staff's children and grandchildren attend school, programs are increasing because they know the programs are needed to make a well-rounded student.

The school board's primary focus is supposed to be concentrated on the budget and student improvement. One can view recordings or live streaming of school board meetings to witness that concentration is mainly on the budget. Most boards are trained by the people throughout this chain to stay focused on the budget, not on academic issues. Because most members are Democrats at the local level, the focus is on adequate funding of teachers' contracts, not on academic performance. I have never been able to figure this out. Over 80% of union staff members do not live in these failing districts and moreover cannot even vote in them.

Now, let us discuss the Charter School Movement that is currently being led by Federal Education Secretary Betsy Devos. People believe a lot of things about her, one being that she uses Black people for the profit of her personal business associates. Keep in mind that the largest industry in America is K–12 education, in which funding is continuous.

Every city in every state has a school, and it is usually the focal point of the community. Schools are the centerpiece, the economic engine for the community. Urban areas provide excellent opportunities for business growth. There are underperforming schools, lack of capital investments, greed, hopes and dreams for a better life, and disinvested principal players. So, you start an alternative educational opportunity called "charter schools" that obtain government funding and can be started in primarily urban areas that are failing at education, but the stakeholders of these schools have an abundance of disinterest in the students and parents of the school.

For decades, stakeholders have lacked solutions and have maintained a monopoly on education in those failing districts. The parents of these students, who are often as equally uneducated, and the voting grandparents, who are often similar to the parents, have been victims of the same inadequate education from the same failing districts.

Seeking something new, the initial entry point into the community was through Black church ministers, whose congregations are declining. The urban members' income isn't keeping pace with inflation, which is causing sharp declines in church revenues. Church buildings provide adequate space to start a school, and the churches get a new revenue source. That is how charter schools get a foothold in Black communities. Just simply share the income with the ministers. When federal programs share the revenue, they almost eliminate resistance from the community.

Public schools continue to fight the battle in the political arena, primarily led by the argument that financial resources are being diverted from public schools to teachers' unions, which pretty much abandoned the urban areas years before. There is a large distance that has grown between stakeholders that include school boards, administrators, staff, state departments of education, and churches and the local public-school stakeholders, including parents and students. Most leadership live, work, and play in the suburbs and have little in common with urban students besides the color of their skin.

Corporate America used that rift and the relationship with Black ministers to gain access to the community. They came into the school districts with new computers and technology that the districts had not previously provided and hired younger, lower-paid staff members that believed that change was needed or that were seeking opportunities to lead in the educational experience earlier in their educational careers.

Charter schools are primarily nonunionized and funded by for-profit agencies. The conclusion in the media is that there were rich and mostly White-owned companies that came into Black communities and took funds away from public schools. The perception is that local communities are damaged economically. Keep in mind that 75–85% of the professional staff usually takes their salaries back to their own suburban communities.

Public schools by far have the fewest number of minority and small vendors that provide services for them. In fact, because of their size, the vendor base is primarily White suburban companies, while charter schools are usually small businesses that use local people. In far more cases than in public schools, charter schools use African American, Hispanic, Asian, or other minority employees. They provide opportunities to lead the schools and provide vending opportunities to small businesses located in urban communities. Also, with Black ministries leading these schools, funds began flowing around Black communities at unprecedented levels. I would go so far as to say that charter schools have been the largest avenue for minority business development in the country. Although urban public-school boards and administrations are primarily run by minorities, they, for the most part, leave minority businesses outside looking in for business opportunities in the school districts. Isn't it something that the Betsy DeVos industry is leading in minority business development and union-dominated traditional public schools' primary vendor base is nonminority suburban vendors? I am not sure why this is a surprise, as most union employees in 2018 lived in the suburbs. I am clearly in support of choice. The primary question is, Why should poor parents be forced to take their children to schools where professional staff will not bring theirs? It is not fair.

What happened in Florida?

The State of Florida has used standardized tests in primary and secondary public schools for quite a few years. One such test was the Florida Comprehensive Assessment Test (FCAT/FCAT 2.0). The tests were not without controversy. The first round of tests was administered statewide in 1998, replacing the State Student Assessment Test (SSAT) and the High School Competency Test (HSCT). These statewide standardized tests were used to determine if children were "qualified" to graduate. It was found that some students that received excellent grades throughout their high school career failed the test and were denied graduation status. Students from poor districts reported that the information on the test was NEVER even covered in class! It is a setup, designed to perpetuate the notion that Blacks are inferior and incapable of learning at the level of Whites.

Imagine that students take a test containing information they have never been taught. As discriminating as that sounds, the reader would think that Whites were still working to make Blacks the permanent underclass. Can you image that the primary individuals in control of the somewhat equally funded school are Black or Brown? It is true. The educators have the same skin color as the students, but little else in common. Is it possible that Black, suburban, middle-class educators are discriminating against Black students? When does the sabotage stop? Intelligent students have been held back, some up to three times. College delay, public humiliation, and defeat weigh heavy on them. It takes amazing determination to keep pushing when the world seems to be against you from the start. Children in the more affluent schools, of course, passed. The materials on the test were taught in their curriculum.

The intent of Brown v. Board of Education was well intended by the Supreme Court, but people continue to find ways to play mind games. It was not until 2014–2015 that the FCAT was replaced in the state of Florida. However, other comprehensive tests are still being used for some grades. How do you determine the damage that was done for all of those years? How many individuals' lives were scarred from such testing?

The original intent of FCAT testing was to determine if students in the fourth grade were eligible to pass on to the fifth grade. In 2001, the "No Child Left Behind Act" was passed by the U.S. Congress. Mandatory testing was moved to the third grade to comply with the act. The only two instances where state or federal statutes required students to pass the FCAT were now in third grade and prior to graduation. The test was given at other grade levels to provide valuable information, on the school as well as on the student.

Isn't it ironic that the "pipeline to prison" also uses data from students in the third grade? Forecasts are made of how many "at-risk" third-grade students there are to determine how many beds will be needed in the jails and prisons in the very near future. Is Brown v. Board of Education yielding the results the Supreme Court had expected? The truth could not be further from what the court case was designed to do.

With all of these things going against them, no wonder children do not see the dream our pre-Brown v. Board of Education forefathers envisioned for them. The system sabotaged the dream, and our children are paying the price. If children become disillusioned in the third grade, how much harder does the system need to work to restore hope for a future being enriched by our educational system, which appears to be strategically stacked against those who find life already an obstacle course filled with time bombs?

Our children do not read statistics and gauge their future goals and plans by what others have said as their reality. However, those in charge of molding their futures often do. As an educator, my job may be to educate Johnny, but have I adopted a reduced expectation of who Johnny can become? If I am his teacher, does this affect the amount of time and energy that I invest in teaching him? Do I get to the point of feeling that it is a waste of my invested time attending college—that I have possibly deluded myself into thinking I can garner one of the better positions?

CHAPTER THREE

When Schools Do Not Make the Grade

PERHAPS IT IS not just the students that feel shortchanged on the goods promised by Brown v. Board of Education. Today, many teachers are teaching in urban schools but have moved to the suburbs. That being the case, how do you suppose urban students can tap into resources after school? Suburban families not only have teachers available that work in their districts but also have the teachers and administrators that work in the urban districts to supplement their local educators. This has had a negative impact on urban districts, where there is no support for students after school. There is no teacher living next door to ask questions if there is homework after school or in the summer months.

Quite often in the news, we see that the first responder to a crime or accident scene is an off-duty professional. Whether it is an off-duty policeman that thwarted a robbery or an off-duty fireman that rescued someone from harm, off-duty professionals are a valuable resource in our neighborhoods. In their own neighborhoods, they volunteer for community events, and organizations benefit from these professionals living in the community. This works the same for off-duty educators. If Johnny is having trouble with math and Mrs. Robinson right next door is a math teacher, Johnny could potentially benefit from a little extra help from his neighbor.

Back in the inner-city neighborhood, Robert does not have the benefit of running into any of his teachers at Walmart or at the gas station. Imagine if two or more of Robert's teachers attended his church or lived a few blocks away. When children see teachers visible in their lives more than just during school hours, a different type of bond is present. Would Johnny be sent to the office for every infraction if the staff actually knew Johnny's family from church or high school? That was the environment for Black children when Brown v. Board of Education was enacted. So, in fact, children's access to quality education has reversed itself in regard to teachers living in their neighborhoods.

One of the most stressful aspects of the teacher's job is dealing with disrespectful and rude students that provide classroom distractions. If children are likely to run into their teacher outside the classroom, they are less likely to act up and would reserve a degree of respect for their teacher. At school, a teacher is just a person in a position. Outside the classroom, they become Mr. Jackson or Ms. Jones; they become real people to the child. A lot of acting up in school is done to show off in front of peers to get the attention they do not receive at home or in the community.

There are other factors that stress children out and are more than likely the reason students enter the classroom with an attitude that has been brewing for some time. Hunger is a major factor with many children in our inner-city schools. A lot of families depend upon the free or reduced-cost lunch program to supplement their children's daily nutrition. It is not uncommon that children come to school on Monday after the weekend, eat breakfast, and get a stomachache because that is the most food they have had since Friday when they left school. The school lunch director and the principal or other school leader on some occasions send unused lunches home with students to eat over the weekend.

Money, or the lack thereof, is a major factor in the lives of many people. There is a cost attached to providing quality education to students. We have lost the education war when we are teaching to a test that we all know puts urban kids at a disadvantage because the developer of the test covers all the racial and gender profiles. What they do not cover is the economic profiles. So, the tests are developed by middle—and upper-class citizens based on their own life experiences. Why would a test be developed with a bias against the economically disadvantaged in our society? Not only is it cruel, but also it is unfair. Why ask students to concentrate on studying for tests that they have limited chances of passing? The consequences of not passing the standardized tests are so devastating that all of the schools' resources have been geared toward preparing students for them, at the cost of eliminating life skills, athletics, and performing arts.

The lack of performance on a test results in an uphill climb at best. Why are the self-appointed leaders not marching for a more even playing field? It is because Black and Brown leadership families are exempt from the struggles of the urban educational experience. Their children's educational lives are primarily in suburban, private, or urban schools (which are private schools within the public school system) that require a passable test to get into.

One of the alternatives, prison, costs money too. What is never factored in is the opportunity cost of those lives that were never afforded the privilege of living up to their full potential. These students earmarked for prison, if they are able to adequately read by the third grade, are never able to return with their talents to enrich the society in which they grew up. On second thought, the society received the return on their investment, the funneling of warm bodies with undernourished potential into the prison system. School boards, administrations, and professional staff are all the same color, but in most cases have nothing else in common with the students under their oversight but skin color. These families deserve better because we know that adequate education is the key to leaving the poverty trap. Brown v. Board of Education petitioners would have never been able to see the integration that is now occurring in nonurban areas of the United States. I am not sure if the Blacks in the nonurban areas would be comfortable with an influx of urban Blacks into their communities. The separation caused by financial differences is a major roadblock to student improvement.

It costs approximately $28,284 a year to incarcerate a prisoner. That is an average of $77 a day per person. Statistics bear out the fact that the high school dropout rate is directly tied to the increase in the prison population. When it comes to young Black men, more than one-half of them that attend high school never earn a high school diploma. Out of that population, 60% are expected to go to prison. The higher the level of education obtained, the lower the risk of criminal activity involvement.

Young Latino men do not fare much better. Latinos and Blacks have the odds stacked against them. When it comes to suspension from school, Black students are three times more likely to be suspended than White students. Latinos, coupled with Blacks, account for 70% of all students arrested in school. Out of the entire prison population, Blacks make up 61% of those incarcerated. The devastating disparity is that of the entire prison population, Blacks number 30% of inmates. Inside prisons, 68% of the population never finished high school, which is a sad report on our educational system.

When you see these statistics, the first thing that comes to mind is the systemic racial bias against young Black and Latino students. The statistic bears out that there must be some racial problem, with these races of people so disproportionately being dismissed from schools. However, it is hard to make that argument because the majority of the senior management and the boards of directors are Black and Brown themselves. So, it is more about economics or community differences than about race. Instead of saying that Black students get suspended at a higher rate, should we actually say that poor children are the victim of suspension, disciplinary actions, and prison? Would not a more accurate reason for why children are treated disproportionately worse be their economic status and not their color?

The United States holds the position of having the largest prison population in the entire world. Prison is the place where poor and uneducated people are disproportionately more likely to consider their residence at some time in their life. Middle-class Black and Brown people are just as unlikely to see the inside of prison walls as Whites if they are not surrounded by poverty and the adverse effects of it. There needs to be a fork in the road. The yellow brick road of promise has been highjacked from our young people. We owe it to them, to Brown, Plessy, Martin Luther King, Jr., Thurgood Marshall, and ourselves and future generations to create a detour to the road to prison and rebuild the vision of my mother and others.

CHAPTER FOUR

The Problem with Title I and Changing Roles

FOR OVER SIXTY years, Title I has been the largest federally funded educational program that supplements school funding for schools that have a higher concentration of students trapped and suffering in poverty. This assistance is meant to help schools meet their educational goals. Schools that receive these supplemental funds are designated as Title I schools.

The basic principle of Title I is that schools with a larger population of low-income students would receive additional funding. This is to ensure that schools have more resources available to provide the programs and additional assistance needed. It has been determined that the number of students applying for and receiving free or reduced-cost lunches could also successfully indicate the number of low-income students that a school has in its enrollment.

So, where can these Title I schools best use these funds? The spectrum is wide, and schools may have flexibility in determining how the funds will be used, depending on what the particular student body needs to support reaching their academic goals.

Title I funds can be used to

- improve curriculum,

- support instructional activities,
- enhance parental involvement,
- provide counseling,
- increase staff,
- improve programs.

Those that benefit from Title I funding include

- students at or below the poverty line,
- migrant students,
- students needing assistance in becoming proficient in English,
- homeless students,
- students with disabilities,
- delinquent students,
- neglected students,
- any at-risk student in need.

In order to maintain this supplemental funding, all you have to do is apply for additional funding based on your state's funding allocation guidelines. Schools have stated goals to make academic improvements on yearly state tests and show how they have focused on best teaching practices. It would appear that Title I should work for disadvantaged students, but is it really working?

In 2014, $14 billion in supplemental funding was provided to states to improve their student achievement levels. Did it work? Studies did not find adequate evidence that there was any significant improvement in students' achievement levels. Is this acceptable? For a program that has been in existence for over sixty years, there should have been ample time to work out the bugs and tweak its effectiveness.

What I find ironic is that Title I funds are determined by how many students qualify for free or reduced-cost school lunches. Is this really an accurate way to determine which children need help? I believe this is an acceptable way to determine funding. Free and reduced-cost lunch students are considered at-risk for educational vulnerabilities. With such a wide range of programs that could be enhanced or implemented with Title I funds, are funds being appropriated in the best way for the sake of the children? In most cases, no, because these are grant funds that are allocated each year regardless of academic performance. So, for the most part, they are handled as funds that are supplemental in nature and where you can get all the people and things that the general fund budget cannot afford but are within the grant guideline.

Or if you have staff you want to protect, placing them in the guaranteed grant allows it to become almost a permanent job. Are the programs that are needed to enhance their education added to the curriculum? Are the necessary technological tools added to their classrooms? Are teachers getting the support they need to increase the children's learning experiences? Unfortunately, the results do not bear witness to any substantial evidence that Title I is reaching the goal it was created to accomplish. What could be the reasons for its apparent failure?

The problem that occurs with any governmental program is that it is set up for the worst among us. Because of abuse over the years, there are very strict guidelines for use of the funds. The record keeping becomes so time-consuming as to take away from instruction. Like most failing programs, it becomes more about the money than about performance.

This is one of those issues where the thought and even the heart are there, but the American way of GREED just slips its way into the system. Let us think about two things. First, the more Title I money a school district gets, the more its programs have to comply with strict federal guidelines. The thing to note is that suburban school districts do not complain about an imbalance of funding. The allocation of Title I funds is primarily under the category of supplemental assistance for students to receive free or reduced-cost lunches. So, in high-poverty areas, there are just substantially more students that meet this standard. Therefore, additional funding is given to those schools.

If there is a multibillion-dollar pot of funds, why are the suburban schools not lobbying for more money since the allocation of those funds is discriminating against the very people that write the Title I program? Most of Title I's writers are highly educated and would more than likely live in America's suburbs, where education is statistically better than in urban America. Stop there and think about that for a second. The people who write the national standards and measures live in the suburbs but make sure that the urban schools continue to get funded. But the schools where their children attend are largely left out of the Title I oversight that urban and rural schools have to adhere to. Does that make any sense?

Yes, it makes sense because it gives the suburban districts the flexibility to implement programs that work. Just remember that "the money is in the failure." So, I can keep extra funding for my professional development trips to some real nice place, get my niece a job as an assistant, and my children can learn comfortably in my suburban community. I am not saying that is what actually happens, but you can see the picture—that it could.

Although you can point to pockets or specific schools within the urban school network that do perform well, let me say this: When I speak of "URBAN America," I am synonymously saying "RURAL America," because the problems in both areas mirror one another.

Affluent Black neighborhoods' academic performance far exceeds that of rural White America. In my opinion, that's what is fueling the phenomenon called Donald Trump. Therefore, you can see that race is not the factor that the public makes it out to be. It is more economics that separates educational opportunities for academic underperformance. White rural and urban citizens see the upward mobility of Black Americans, which provokes frustration because the lack of educational opportunities is also affecting rural Americans trapped in the Title I hole. The president has been able to tap into that frustration in rural and urban White America.

If you think about it, the phenomenon defies conventional wisdom. If I am at the table writing the Title I program, I am going to make sure that there is something in it for me. Now let us take it further. The more federal Title I funding you get, the worse the school performs. With the least amount of Title I funding you receive, the better you perform. On the face of it, the "school improvement grant" is a noncompetitive grant that is given to schools just for being poor. The rich school districts' mothers and fathers write the program parameters but write themselves out of it because they are disadvantaged, which sounds pretty fishy on the surface.

No one takes into account that when school improvement grants provide no provision for successfully achieving benchmarks in urban schools, they might lose funding because of new grants for underperforming schools. How can that be? Remember, "THE MONEY IS IN FAILURE." The people that write the program are also the people that have friends that provide the experimental programs and new education theories that are tried on urban and rural children, and not on suburban children.

The less the amount of Title I funding you receive, the more educational flexibility you have, and the less amount of paperwork and reporting you have to contend with. Because it is a grant, the string attached to Title I is the reporting on all data about all the poor kids and their families in America. So, if I am writing the grant, I will exempt my family from the data collection and concentrate the reporting and data collection on poor citizens.

Statistical data is valuable to land developers, prison operators, hospitals, and other entities. That is why you hear in educational circles that third grade is a critical time for children to be education-ally successful. If you look at at-risk children that cannot read in the third grade, their special education learning disables their likelihood of being in the prison pipeline. If you believe the Tuskegee Syphilis Experiment was a scam, can you image having access to the poor fam-ilies in America and being able to experiment and perform research on them annually to make money for your family and friends? If you have an experimental program that you can get adopted, you have a $15 billion grant that will almost be mandated, and you're in all fifty states. Additionally, if you need extra money, you can get a specific federal grant for the worst-performing schools where you can even concentrate deeper on the lives of these poor students and their families.

If you keep these students underperforming, you have a con-tinuous and cheap labor source. Let's take this even further. You set a system up that is based on statistics so you can manage a school district from the comfort of your own home or a country club, and nobody is the wiser.

In sports, we have fantasy football. The best fantasy football player is never given a coaching position, but in education, fantasy educators can run a whole district of poor students. A fantasy football player never coached in the National Football League, college, or high school. It is because a statistical approach does not take into account the human aspect and the differences in personalities.

If things are this bad, why are more people besides a small-time CPA from Michigan not coming forward and blowing the whistle on this complete violation of privacy inherent in the nonperforming grant and its nationwide negative impact on poor people in America? I will explore each of these points.

You may have heard of a document called the "school improvement plan." This is the document that is supposed to guide schools' academic performance. It is the academic business plan of the district. Although districts' budgets, staffing levels, professional development, and programming are derived from this document, it is very rarely discussed at the school board or public level. I would go further to say that most school boards probably have never seen this document that is supposed to be the academic business plan of the district. How is it that the document, which is the plan to improve academic performance, is not discussed, reviewed, or argued about? The school improvement plan is supposed to be the guiding force behind the improved performance of students in all districts across the country, and one of the requirements of the Title I grant is to follow the school improvement plan.

The higher the number of free and reduced-cost lunch students that a district has, the more control the school improvement plan and grants have over the academic, professional development, and operation of the schools. The school improvement plan is similar to President Obama's signature program called "Race to the Top." The basis of this program is that if you implement these national standards, then you can compete for the funds. The more you implement the proposed national development standards, the more you can be in the "Race to the Top" funding sweepstakes. If you do not compete but still implement the program without the funding, you are eligible to compete in round two for the funding. Well, that essentially is Title I. If you implement this national experimental approach, then you can receive the funds. However, you have to have a school improvement plan. You do not need the school board or curriculum committee approval; you only need state approval for the grant. You need no public discussion of how your performance is, as compared to grant goals. That is unlike the situation with the budget, where appropriations need to be approved by the school board. There needs to be public input. There are usually a lot of discussion and sometimes even strikes because the budget does not meet the requirements of school stakeholders. So, if you use the "tone at the top" approach to managing schools, then you can see that finances, not academics, become the focal point of the school.

Federal government

In 1965, the Elementary and Secondary Education Act (ESEA Pub.I.89-1—Stat 27, 20 USC ch. 70) launched a comprehensive set of programs, including the Title I program, giving federal aid to the disadvantaged. The act funds primary and secondary education while explicitly forbidding the establishment of a national curriculum. As mandated in the act, the funds are authorized for professional development, instructional materials, and resources that support educational programs and promote parental involvement. The act was originally authorized through 1970; however, the government has authorized the act every five to ten years since its initial enactment. The current reauthorization of ESEA is called the No Child Left Behind Act of 2001 (NCLB). NCLB also allows military recruiters to access eleventh- and twelfth-grade students' names, addresses, and telephone numbers when requested. As an offshoot of the anti-poverty movement, Title I was enacted in 1965.

The Brown v. Board of Education legislation was key to this grant program. As new administrations have come through the White House and Congress, the intent of the program has remained the same, but the effectiveness continues to be in question, and who profits from the grant is even more in question. Most urban and rural districts, where funds are scarce, depend on these funds for their livelihoods. This became the stick to get poor districts to implement programs that become profit centers for vendors and give unproved businesses money in isolated situations. You have the same group or maybe even just one school in one city successfully implementing a program that improves academic performance or higher performance on standardized testing for a group of poor children. If you know people in the right place, it can be the national standard by being included in the national standards in the Title I grant. Then that and connection to the current administration become the national standard for poor children around the country.

In 1954, when Brown v. Board of Education was litigated, funding from the federal government was most often awarded for special programs such as vocational education. Keep in mind that all the data that is currently collected on students is gathered and submitted to the federal government for analysis, with the objective of improving education on a national basis. As anti-poverty programs were set up by people that understood and resided in the urban neighborhoods, they could assist in creating programs that improved the circumstances of urban and rural citizens.

There was no diversity in housing, and the more affluent, regardless of color and gender, were primarily residents of the financially segregated parts of the urban section of towns but attended the local schools. The interaction between the economic classes of Blacks has now been separated by zip code. Where are the children of the doctors, accountants, lawyers, and business owners that attended these schools with the working class and the poor in 1954, if these communities are now segregated more by economics than by race?

Realize that it has been two or three generations since the integration of public schools. The higher-educated Blacks that have little to nothing in common with the neighborhood people of color, other than the color of their skin, are at the decision table. This means that impoverished or at-risk students have no representation at the decision table. How does that occur? I will explore the stakeholders individually. The reflection of how they were affected THEN and how they are affected NOW.

State government

State governments have a role that has always been as an intermediary. This is the perfect position, with the control to modify grants and to fund positions within the state government through overhead cost reimbursement. They have the ability to amend grants and administer them, within federal guidelines, if they stay in compliance with the hiring of federally approved vendors. By adopting federally approved goals, states realize that the less pushback you give, the less likely you are to have your funding reduced or have to deal with federal oversight for noncompliance with the grant's goal to improve education.

In fact, the worse the schools perform and the worse job you do to improve education, the more funding you receive. They are in a perfect position—all the control and no public accountability. The funding provides supplements to state budgets and gives the state more actual control over the academic performance of schools. The documents they review and approve usually are never seen by boards of directors; they are created 100% for implementation purposes. This is the qualification for those that review these grants, which basically control our average-paid governmental employees.

Funding that was given out to low-performing schools was SEG funding, which provided schools with additional money for programs that were beyond the normal programming. The normal funding requirement is that you maintain the programs within the grant without additional funding. These funds go away if you successfully implement these programs and scores improve. This additional funding was given for a period of time to improve educational performance, and the recipients could do creative things with the funding. Districts could extend the school day, add additional student aides, or spend the money in other areas that were identified as needed by the administration.

I personally worked at a school that received SEG funds and subsequently chose to start the high school day at 6:00 in the morning. School enrollment went from 400+ students to 145 students, which caused irreparable financial harm to the school. It was effectively taken over by the State of Michigan and closed. The students then had to be sent to other districts for educational opportunities. No one even discussed the state's role or the consulting firm that supported the recommendation that earned approximately $500,000 in consulting fees. But it was the board of directors in front of the microphone that the public was led to believe was the cause of the district's failure.

Although states have control over academic programs, Title I funding parameters control the majority of the educational programs. States approve the use of the funds, but take no responsibility for the success or failure of the program. They lack any public accountability.

You would think that for underperforming schools, you would get the best consultant to work with the school board and administrators to improve academic performance. The problem is that most consultants do not have a successful history of academically improving underperforming schools. So, if the school doesn't perform, there are plans to take control of it through management changes in the school board agreement, charterization, etc. But the same person that was approved and working with the schools maintains their position with little or no accountability. Keep in mind that the state official gets approval and indirect control over the school through the grant process, with no accountability for performance or outcome. On the other side, the board of education, which is fully accountable for academic performance, almost never sees or approves the school improvement plan.

Board of director

School board members have always been required to live within the district's city, township, or county where the school is located. For the most part, the board members in the urban areas of the city were more diverse than in the suburban areas, yet they were still controlled by a White majority. Segregation was by area of the city, but schools were divided by race. In the smaller cities where the majority was Black and Brown, they controlled the education and the makeup of the boards, but there was a division between working-class and professional citizens.

This was also true of larger southern cities with larger majority populations. The boards of education were split along socioeconomic lines. There, the boards concentrated on community development and job readiness. Skilled trades were a staple for the workforce, and only 25% of the students left school headed for college. Because most of the skilled trades and district operations were performed by contractors from within the district, the workers that maintained the district's facilities were primarily from within the community.

As time has gone by, the makeup of the boards of education in urban and rural areas has almost exclusively changed to college-educated people within the community. They have educational backgrounds on paper but have few ties to the actual students and parents they serve in the majority of poor districts. Their ties are more closely aligned with the teachers' union, and teachers and principal administrators do more socializing through college relationships and other social organizations than with community members. This has become a problem, because in most urban areas, the success and failure of a district are based on a model that is developed by and administrated by people with a higher education, which accounts for only 30% or fewer of the parents.

The advent of standardized tests gave them justification to concentrate on testing that has had little or no effect on the lives of college-bound students. As the boards become so concentrated with college-educated members, their singular focus is college, so the majority of the financial resources are directed at those students. Students that want alternative career paths are all but left out of the decision-making.

The value set of the elected body is concentrated on higher education and standardized tests that do not reflect the abilities of non-college-bound students. Therefore, the school board, which holds the keys to the operation, has a focus on college-bound students, and there is no one in the room who represents the students and families that are not interested in college, but rather are interested in obtaining employability skills. Because decision-makers have eliminated the skilled trades or employability curriculum, there has been a negative material impact on entrepreneurs within the urban community, which has caused an employment gap.

Urban schools do not teach students how to live in the world, but rather concentrate all their time and effort on test-taking skills. The irony is that they do not do a good job of concentrating resources on professional staff and simple things that would assist in classroom performance.

The students in the suburbs, for the most part, have had access to computers, which is where the digital gap was exposed during the COVID-19 lockdown. Keep in mind that students have to take standardized tests on computers, but some do not have access or experience with computer keyboards and applications that are timed and monitored. Most urban students' primary mode of communication is the cellular phone, which has a keyboard, but typing is done with the user's thumbs. So, when it comes to taking a standardized test on a computer with a keyboard, it puts even people with a minimal knowledge base at a disadvantage.

Keep in mind that the school improvement plan doesn't need the district board's approval, and most people do not know the district's education strategy. The concentration is primarily on the budget and contract approval. In most suburban districts, the school board does not have programs that include local vendors in the contract process, but manage to concentrate most of the business opportunities on local vendors, whereas in urban districts, although they have a majority of Blacks and Browns on the board, the opportunities given to companies that look like them are lacking and are probably the most lopsided in any governmental unit. That is a 180-degree turn from the time Brown v. Board of Education was enacted. The primary vendors for districts where minorities controlled the voting selected minority firms to provide the needed services.

Principal administrators

When Brown v. Board of Education was litigated, not only was equal funding of schools a major issue, but also adequate pay for principal administrators in Black communities, whose pay was substantially below that of their White counterparts, was an issue. Urban administrators primally lived in the communities, and their children attended the same schools as the children they administrated. They personally knew the parents and worked with the families to ensure that the children had employability skills, whether it was via college or via the trades, such as plumbing or mechanics.

Fast-forward to 2020. It is rare for any of the urban principal administrators to live in the districts where they are employed. This takes away from the direct connection to urban parents, and their skills are being used in communities where their own children are being educated. There is a need for additional resources because a fact of life is that less affluent students cost more to educate. The reason being is that their basic needs for food, shelter, and attention are not always being met.

Most urban districts are underfunded for the needs of the students because they lack the financial support of the parents, due to the parents' own lack of resources. Contrast that with some of the suburban districts. If funding for athletics is reduced or reallocated to the classroom, parents usually fill in the gaps, whereas in urban areas, those resources are usually not as available, so the children go without or just quit the sport they love because they cannot afford the gear needed to participate in the sport. Because data is the root of education analysis, there are many reports that look at everything that centers around the use of financial resources, which is a regulatory burden.

Administrators have limited resources, disconnection from the community, and students learning testing materials that are not useful in their lives. As can be expected, the turnover rate in these positions is high. The expectations of the position are almost impossible to meet, and administrators have a life with their own children in another district with another whole set of racial, financial, and ethnic issues that also take their full concentration.

Moving students to achieve integration is not always successful inside or outside the classroom. The limited amount of socialization has their children's views and way of life questioned because of the difference in skin color. As a student myself that was primarily in advanced placement classes with very few Blacks, I was limited in my social interactions. Because I did not know any of the students personally, there was no one to call to ask about a homework question. This kind of social isolation sometimes has negative effects on students in suburban schools, which means that administrators have to keep an eye on their children and grandchildren to ensure they are well adjusted.

Some students rebel with the suburban rebels and take the same path of trouble, following them in the suburban schools. In addition, conforming to the suburban way of life brings the thought that you are not like the Blacks on television and a feeling of nonacceptance in either urban or suburban settings, which takes a toll on some students.

Students with a parent that is a school administrator have "educational credit," because most administrators have relationships with their own children and understand what students should be getting in an educational setting. To maintain that "education credit," you have to be involved in your children's lives, because as an educator, you know how important that is to grow as a student and person. Although you are well-meaning, you have the need to ensure that your own children are well adjusted. However, participation with the parents and/or students at your own children's schools pulls you away from the district in which you work. When they were one and the same, this problem did not exist to such an extent.

All the staff turnover and the lack of full-time community interaction puts the administrator at a disadvantage with community needs issues. By the time the administrator gets more involved in the community, they're headed to another district, so usually they are implementing national best practices and never getting to retrofit those practices to the local community. This situation was different for the years between 1954 and the late 1970s to early 1980s when administrators were full-time residents of the community and their children attended school in the districts where they held administrative positions. In 1954, 75% of administrators lived in the districts they served. By the early 1980s, that figure was only 25%.

Teachers

Teachers followed the same pattern. They moved to the suburbs and began sending their own children to suburban schools.

Question

Is it possible to promote or believe in a product that you will not use yourself? If urban schools are not good enough for 75% of the people that directly deliver education, is it good enough for the students they serve?

As I think of teachers, I think about my aunt Lauie Githiri, who taught in the Fort Wayne Community Schools for over thirty years. She marched with Martin Luther King for civil rights in the 1960s. She came to Fort Wayne, finished her education, and lived with our family while completing her studies. Her first student was me. I was somewhere between three to five years old at the time when Aunt Lauie taught me the alphabet and how to count to one hundred before I started kindergarten. This put me at the head of the class, and I have worked my whole life to remain in that position.

But it was more to my point. In the 1950s, teachers and administrators lived in the neighborhoods and communities where they served. The primary reason for this was that communities were segregated along racial lines. The compensation for teachers, administrators, and other workers was less in communities of color than in the communities of their White counterparts. There were also differences in materials and facilities.

Schools that were primarily for Black, Brown, and poor Whites set the primary goal for students to be able to fill labor jobs. That was at a time when people actually worked, and they lived in the communities where they worked. School staff didn't have the level of compensation of their White counterparts, but the communities placed great confidence in and support for those individuals, up to and including providing free food, places to stay, and repairs to their cars and homes at below cost. The communities at that time understood that the best way to a better life was through education.

Getting qualified as education professionals was needed to improve the options for their children. They wanted their children to have a better life than they had. They wanted to escape the backbreaking labor and domestic jobs that a vast majority of the communities were limited to. The sense of being a teacher was like the sense of being a civil rights leader, because teachers were tasked with leading the community out of the academic bondage that continued to plague the Black community. The community celebrated educational achievement. The teachers that lived in the communities could talk with parents that were not tolerant of unruly activities in the school buildings. If you were a principal and students did not show up for class, you would send somebody from the school to get in touch with the parents to assist them in making sure their children attended and received the lessons.

The little-discussed fact related to the Brown v. Board of Education suit was the area that addressed the inequity in funding for teacher and administrative salaries. The most discussed was the inequity in funding for school operations, and there was just as much concentration on teacher and administrative wage inequities.

As the integration of housing in America started to slowly take hold, the first families to take advantage were teachers' families. The unequal wages issue was being addressed, teachers were starting to get more opportunities to teach in nonurban districts, and they were some of the first accepted in White communities.

Fast-forward to 2020, when less than 20% of education professionals live in the urban communities where they work. The demographics of the teaching ranks changed as the paths of opportunity for positions increased and diversified from the 1950s and 1960s. A large majority of professionals opted for teaching positions because other professional occupations were slower to integrate. As opportunities outside education opened up, more people switched to more lucrative professions. So, wages increased and in some cases exceeded the rural and suburban district education professionals' wages. Non-Blacks started taking those vacated education jobs, and Blacks also got opportunities in suburban majority White districts. As time passed, the percentage of professionals that lived in the school districts they served declined from almost 100% to less than 20%. The number of professionals that actually take their children to those schools now is even less than that.

This brings up the question of how you can promote an operation that you yourself would not use. So, with the advent of teachers and other education professionals moving to the suburbs, there is now a concentration of educators in the suburbs and an education desert in urban areas. The teachers brought additional skills that supported the PTAs and provided more tutors and educational resources. Urban districts, with their larger budgets, provide teachers with the latest cutting-edge educational techniques, because there is always a push for higher performance. Professional development courses not only benefit local districts but also provide guidance for the communities during parent-teacher conferences and assist in other programs, including field trips, athletics, and summer community programs, which are all part of the full educational program.

In 1950, for example, if you were studying for a test and needed assistance with a question, you could ask your next-door neighbor mom or dad who was a teacher in the same urban district where you both lived. In 1950, that situation was available to Black children. In 2020, it isn't, because the urban areas where Black children live are now education deserts.

I will conclude with another problem, which is the shortage of teachers throughout the United States. There has been a steady decrease over the years, but it has taken a sharp drop over the past five years. Republicans have taken control, and the new wave is to grade teachers on the academic performance of their students. Data goes into a database so that other educators can see prior student performance. As this becomes more prevalent, the number of seasoned teachers declines at a rapid pace in urban areas.

You may ask, "Why?" It is because if my personal grade is based on student performance, then I will retire prior to getting evaluated. Knowing that these children stand little chance of performing satisfactorily based on the level of education that is going on and it will hurt my reputation as an educator, I am retiring. The teachers, to their credit, have limited control over their environment, and the lack of connection with the families gives them a feeling of hopelessness. They think, *I want to do more, but I have to follow the contract, which could lead to peer pressure to discontinue the assistance.*

You have to understand that most teachers' contracts are written to protect the worst and lowest-performing staff members. There is usually no or limited compensation for outstanding staff members. The outstanding or the harder-working staff get paid the same as the ineffective staff, so one has to question, "Why continue?" This has limited impact on suburban schools but leaves large numbers of openings at urban schools.

Most states have developed alternate routes to a teaching certificate. Now, primarily underemployed or unemployed individuals can get accepted into a certification program, be given certified teacher duties and responsibilities, and be paid while still in training. They are qualified as certified teachers to ensure that federal and state guidelines can be met. The adult can achieve compliance, but the students that need the most help get the least-qualified education service provider. Does that sound like the way to improve educational outcomes? No.

Parents

One of the prayed for decisions of the Black community was the Brown v. Board of Education decision. Finally, parents could get what had been escaping them since slavery. This was the belief that education was the key for their children to become better prepared to have access to higher-paying jobs that required formal education. It would allow the masses of Blacks to cross over to jobs and professions that were almost exclusively White-dominated. This would give Blacks different opportunities besides the backbreaking labor that had been the center of Black earning power since the end of slavery.

The Black family was primarily made up of the man in the family, who was the primary breadwinner, and the wife, who would sometimes work outside the home. Many would work as domestics, assisting White women with housework and the caretaking of the children. At home, they would keep the family unit together, ensuring the family was adequately fed and clothed.

The 10–15% of students that were lucky enough to obtain a formal college education at one of the Black colleges were concentrated in jobs that serviced the Black community. These jobs included doctors, lawyers, nurses, school teachers, and undertakers and were needed so the Black community could act as a separate but unequal community. Members of the community would also hire outside business people that could provide primary services and make minor repairs, because there was a lack of capital access and contract opportunities to fund businesses that could actually hire people from within the community.

The dream was that schools would be equally funded and Black students would get the same opportunities in the classroom as White students. Parents would march and hold meetings to support this effort and to ensure that students had the hoped-for opportunities. They would make sure that students were at school. If a student's behavior was disrupting the class, a telephone call or a discussion at church with the parent would ensue. The student's attention would increase, and distractions at home would be addressed. Do not get me wrong; there were parents that would not fully support the teacher, but other parents would step in to make sure their own child got the opportunity to learn. At that time, the majority of homes had both parents living in the home.

If you fast-forward to 2020, the percentage of Black homes that have both parents is less than 30%. The percentage of Black youth that attends college is approximately 28%. Mothers with outside jobs and those that stay at home with the children are currently the primary breadwinners. For Black men, incarceration, homelessness, joblessness, and hopelessness are at an all-time high.

This was the primary effect of public housing, where mothers with children qualify for the federal Section 8 voucher program that subsidizes housing costs for the mother and, in rare cases, the father. One of the rules of the program was that the father could not live in the home. Many Black male children lack the structure of a father figure in the home. In a lot of cases, they are subject to a "substitute father," a boyfriend or significant other that lives with or frequents the house of the child and provides supervision or guidance without being formally married to the mother. This arrangement is sometimes temporary in nature because the arrangement is usually easily dissolved. In some cases, these arrangements can number in the teens or just one in the life of the child. This can lead to a stability issue for the child.

The relationship among Blacks has become complicated with the change in roles of the breadwinner. Let us explore what has happened to create a change in the home. The Black male child in a single-parent home is asked to take on the adult male role in the family during his childhood days. In poor communities, this puts a lot of pressure on the child to provide resources for the family. In the more suburban communities, that male child has the adult role without actually having to assume the responsibility of being a breadwinner. These are generalizations but only meant to show how different modified families look. In the case of a substitute father, relationships can be fluid. Substitute fathers can come and go because relationships are volatile with the change in the breadwinner in Black households. This is not an exaggeration; it is not as normal in professional, college, or business-owner households because of the difference in household resources.

Women are graduating from college at an estimated ratio of seven women to one man. So, there are more professional women. Although they got a slower start, currently, Black women by far outnumber Black men in the professional workplace. This in turn gives women more financial resources. In poor neighborhoods, women have total dominance over men.

With the implementation of social programs that help poor families with subsistence living, the federal government provides everything a woman needs, except companionship. The federal programs provide food, shelter, cash assistance, medical care, and other support, which largely eliminates the need for the male figure in the house. Most of these programs go so far as to prohibit an adult male from living in the home. This rule is loosely enforced but can be enforced, if necessary. Even if the rule is not enforced, it is always in the back of the minds of the whole family and undermines the adult male's authority or apparent authority in the household.

As you can see, the family unit is vastly different than it used to be, but the situation for college-bound students is still approximately the same, based on the increase in population. The levels of illiteracy, incarceration, teen pregnancy, and truancy have all drastically increased.

Children-improved education

In this chapter, we have explored the Title I grant, which had the intent of improving education. But the grant failure rate for improving educational opportunities is high. The funds are more commonly used to control education at poor schools. The more a district's children are affected by the grant, the more likely there will be a higher academic failure rate. This can be seen more clearly in successful schools that receive less grant funding and have more control over their curriculum and educational opportunities.

The higher the percentage of free and reduced-cost lunch students that attend school in a district, the more control federal and state governments have over day-to-day activities at the schools. However, communities with high poverty rates desperately need funds. Therefore, they continue to accept the funding and comply with rules and regulations that non-Title I schools are mostly free from. The irony is that school board members, administrators, and teachers recognize that the additional burden of these funds makes it almost impossible for student learning. So, they take their children and grandchildren to the districts with the least amount of Title I funding.

As you can see, the federal and state authorities that oversee these schools continue to approve grants without academic improvement restrictions, and they continue to be employed in those positions until retirement. It is clear that accountability at that level is limited, and this makes for a perfect storm. The more funds you distribute, the more control you can extend over poor districts. You can use the data to estimate the number of jails, mental institutions, low-income housing, etc. that a community requires. As is apparent from previous pages, all the stakeholders and the government officials have removed themselves and their families from the academic hurricane so the chance of someone standing up for these children is limited at best.

The most amazing thing is that almost all of the people that are directly overseeing the educational process are indirectly not affected, because they have removed their families from those schools and communities. In fact, because the grant funds are so needed in impoverished communities to maintain their own salaries and contracts, they are turning a blind eye to the devastation that it is having on the communities. You do not even have to turn a blind eye, because they do not really see or feel it because of themselves not living in the communities with at-risk students that attend these schools.

This became clear to me, as the state of Michigan has a partnership district model program that assists the bottom 5% of the school districts and charter schools in the state. As the schools in the School of One program I managed entered the program, there was funding called 21H, which was designed like Title I funding, but it came from the state of Michigan. The thought behind the program was to give qualifying schools extra funds to fill their financial gaps, in order to improve academic performance. One thing I observed that was striking was that Black-controlled schools were lining up for the funding, while White-controlled schools were declining the funding and its inherent control. That's when I started to observe and come to understand why suburban schools were not complaining that their federal Title I funding was vastly less than their urban competitors' funding.

In conclusion, it is clear why educational and community leaders are abandoning urban schools for the suburbs, given the current understanding of how Brown v. Board of Education is applied today with different school demographics than in 1954. Black females have become the dominant family breadwinners. The changing of the breadwinner in Black and Brown households has caused major turmoil. This situation has led to the odds of urban students having a better life declining rapidly, making it more probable that they are facing a lifetime of poverty. Higher education and trade skills are needed to improve their life's trajectory.

Many urban students lack the ability to read adequately, comprehend the reading, and write about what they comprehend. It is almost impossible for these individuals to climb out of the poverty quagmire. It has become increasingly difficult for them, because for women that receive public assistance during their childbearing years, when public assistance ends, they must take entry-level jobs where they are stuck until they retrain themselves or move on to social security. This increases the competition for the lower-wage jobs that students need when they leave school and results in the demand for these jobs staying high and wages staying low.

Schooling is worse now for poor Blacks than it was in 1954 when Brown v. Board of Education was enacted. The only difference now is that the poverty trap is managed by Black people. Impoverished students cannot point to discrimination because the failing schools are primarily controlled by Black leadership. However, the funding level has improved, if you consider the addition of federal funding.

The role teacher unions play

The truth is that unions advocate for the teachers. They are not in the business of making sure students learn or advance. Unions benefit by having as many teachers on their rosters as possible. Why? Because teachers pay union dues. Teachers build their own union organization. A powerful union is built with the number of people they have in their membership.

What has happened with some of the Title I money in the past is that instead of putting the money into tools that enhance the children's ability to reach their educational goals, the money was used to add more teachers, and not necessarily qualified teachers, "to deliver a higher level of service that would increase the students' chances of reaching their educational goals." Unions simply hired more teachers, neither the best nor the brightest, but simply "another dues-paying member."

There are many people creating new schemes and making money on Title I programming. If they are able to successfully pass their programs on the federal level, they can expect carte blanche across the country: complete freedom to act as they think best. Title I has proved to be nothing more than an experiment similar to the Tuskegee Syphilis Experiment. If it fails, it doesn't really matter to those making the decisions, as they never expected much from the recipient population in the first place. Title I is a supplemental income to the "suburbanites," but nothing more than a stranglehold to the "Black/Brown and poor Whites." They do not get a representative share; they just get a representative.

The unethical study

Between 1932 and 1972, an unethical clinical study was conducted on Negro males. The study's purpose was to observe how well these males fared with untreated syphilis. These men were lied to and told that they would be receiving free health care from the U.S. government. A historically Black college within the heart of Alabama was chosen to carry out this unethical crime. Enrolled were 600 poor African American sharecroppers from Macon County, Alabama, and at least 399 of these men had contracted the disease (syphilis) prior to the study; 201 of the men never had the disease. This study was scheduled to only last six months and included free medical care, meals, burial insurance, and the like. However, this scheme lasted for over forty years! None of the men were actually treated. The lie was that they had "bad blood." Unfortunately, this is not the only incident where Blacks were used as guinea pigs. For the sake of pure research, our children continue to suffer.

If you really want to get money for the people that need it, our program works. Pay people to succeed. Regenerate a culture similar to that in my mom's day, where education was important and everyone played a vital part. We have to put the power and money in the hands of those that can make a difference on a day-to-day basis, and not just for unionized members.

CHAPTER FIVE

The C. L. Moore Pay-for-Performance Model

THERE ARE A number of books that explain how bad things were and still are for Black and Brown people in the United States. There is no magic wand that can be waved to solve all of the problems in urban or rural areas, but we are going to review an innovative model that will tackle the real bottom line in education.

I believe that the primary focus of education should be on staff compensation, for staff directly involved with improving education. The level of a child's knowledge should not be based on test scores, as testing does not indicate actual mastery. Students need life skills, such as how to cook, fix things around the house, balance a checkbook, and open a business, to name a few. Instead, schools concentrate on college preparation skills. Just to get into a suburban model school within an urban school district, they separate the students by having them take an entrance exam. I work in a school in the Detroit area, and one of the staff member's child passed the examination and was accepted into the suburban model school that had a long tradition of sending students to college. I thought the family had won the lottery, as it was such a joyous occasion. This is an educational fact: everyone gets paid whether the children learn or not.

Since a large majority of professional staff members live outside the community and have a mostly professional relationship with the students, children that lack the same personal relationships that suburban students have with most of their school staff members are at a major disadvantage. The ability to see staff members at church, at the grocery store, at the mall, or just in the neighborhood is such a benefit. What an advantage if you're studying for a test and you are friends with one of your teachers' children. You can call and ask a question about the big test tomorrow. That's a luxury that urban children lack during their whole educational careers. Educational settings are where some of the most personal relationships that youths have in their formative years occur. These early relationships are very important. That is why, for the most part, schools with at least 65% of their professional staff living in the community where they teach have the highest-performing students. In communities where less than 20% of the staff live in the communities where they teach, you have, for the most part, the lowest-performing schools.

I am convinced from discussions with educators over the years that a lot of the discipline problems are centered around two issues. First, a child that is behind and is disruptive in class can be singled out to perform some academic task in front of the class that he or she is incapable of performing. The student acts up and is dismissed from the classroom. Get the child to forgo embarrassment in front of peers, and the teacher gets rid of a problem. The second is that the student wants to be close to the Black people in the office that they look up to, and they only get a chance to know if they are sent to the office.

The second issue that corresponds to low test performance is the level of Title I funding. I believe this is the situation with education because everyone, including the school boards, administrations, unions, and consultants, makes more money if schools remain in crisis. Is that why the standards change every six months? Whenever urban districts get close to performing adequately, the rules change.

Through my years of working with various schools, I have developed a model that works. This is an administrative incentive approach that is set up to increase salary and benefits, which will be linked directly to increasing student count. It should be linked to the source of increased funding. Most school districts nationwide are tied to funding models based on student count. So, you can tie your school to that funding model. This is really a profit-sharing model.

The primary reason for developing this model is that compensation for children in poor and disadvantaged neighborhoods has to be increased drastically and that America is set up on the premise of risk-reward. One of the only industries where this isn't true is education.

If you work in a district where compensation for teachers and professional staff is the same across the district, you might be teaching at a school with between 10% and 100% at-risk population. If you use the concept of "RISK/reward," it would make sense that a school's staff with a population of students that are 100% at-risk would teach their students to perform well on the standards tests that have been developed to assess the comprehension of the students and the retention of the material they have learned during the school year. Teachers at these schools should get paid more because the higher degree of difficulty in teaching at-risk students.

The current situation is that everyone gets paid the same whether or not they take on the challenging job of teaching children at schools in urban or rural areas with high levels of at-risk students. The one exception is at public schools where students have to be tested to enroll at the school. Those schools would be excluded from this model because they lower the risk by testing and filtering out of the higher-risk students. If your school is concentrated on students with the highest risk for success, then you should be excluded from participation.

This incentive model gives all the staff financial rewards for student enrollment. It also provides the lower-wage bus drivers, aides, and custodians the ability to make extra money using their community relationships to increase enrollment. They would get compensated for that. Usually, there are very few teachers that get the enrollment incentive because they lack the community relationships that bolster enrollment. Once the pool of funds is set, the whole school can participate in the success of the student, based on the contribution noted in your performance appraisal. The incentive plan can be modified based on the state or district within the state.

71

One of the hidden gems that staff understand is that salary increases are directly tied to revenue increases. Then, unions and their staff start to understand that raises aren't automatic. I have said before that a district can have the best academic performance and declining student population, which will still cause downward salary adjustments. Please see the table below for an example.

Example A

Education incentive

- Teachers are paid 9% at the end of the year after final evaluations.
- Three levels of incentives:

Highly effective total of 65% of the incentive pool
Effective total of 35% of the incentive pool
Ineffective total of 0% of the incentive pool

- Incentives will be paid to qualifying employees over the summer in four (4) installments.
- The incentive pool will increase, decrease, or remain the same based on student count.
- Education incentives cannot exceed $5,000 for qualified staff members for the first one hundred students. If the student count increase exceeds one hundred students, the maximum amount per qualified staff member is $7,500.

Example B

Job performance incentive

- Paid at the end of the school year after final evaluations. The support staff is 3%.
- Three levels of incentives:

Highly effective total of 65% of the incentive pool
Effective total of 35 of the incentive pool
Ineffective total of 0% of the incentive pool

- Incentives will be paid out to qualifying employees over the summer in four (4) installments.
- Incentive pool will increase, decrease, or remain the same based on student count.
- Job performance inventive cannot exceed $2,500 for qualified staff members for the first one hundred students. If the student count increase exceeds one hundred students, the maximum amount per qualified staff member is $3,750.

Example C

Enrollment incentive

The enrollment incentive for this program is to increase existing enrollment by 8%. Incentives will be paid in November of the school year. As with the other incentive programs, there are three (3) levels of incentives:

Highly effective recruiters total of 65% of the incentive pool
Effective recruiters total of 35% of the incentive pool
Ineffective recruiters total of 0% of the incentive pool

Highly effective recruiters

- Recruited seven or more previously unenrolled students
- Participated in 85% of the recruiting activities, including attending three or more community events

Effective recruiting

- Recruited two or more previously unenrolled students

- Participated in 60% of the recruiting activities, including attending two or more community events

Ineffective recruiter

Staff will fall into the *ineffective recruiter* category if they enroll fewer than two previously unenrolled students for the year.

In an effort to increase enrollment, there will be a number and variety of recruiting activities held throughout the school year. The school will also participate in a number of community events. Those desiring to take part in the bonuses need to participate in more than 60% of the hosted recruiting activities. Additionally, they need to attend at least two of the school-sponsored community events.

Overview

- Recruited fewer than two previously unenrolled students
- Participated in less than 60% of the recruiting activities
- Attended fewer than two community events

I have worked in the educational arena for the past twenty years as a certified public accountant (CPA). I have worked with charter schools, public schools, and private schools and have witnessed first-hand the decline in the graduation rates in certain school districts and the failure of the educational system as we know it.

The gaps between school districts can vary substantially between low-income and higher-income districts, despite the implementation of Brown v. Board of Education. This model tied revenue to per-formance, and the schools where it has been used have seen up to a 60% increase in student enrollment and an increase in funding for the school. The academic results have been mixed, based on the high level of management turnover, and other districts used it to drive enrollment because they had academic incentives already in place. The model gives the school board and management the ability to enact a pay-for-performance model.

Example of Compensation

			Number of individuals who qualify	Total Compensation per individual
Base Student	$	210.00		
New Blend student count	$	260.00		
Net New Students	$	50.00		
State Aide amount	$	7,800.00		
Total New State Aide	$	390,000.00		
Teacher Education Incentive 7%	$	27,300.00		
Highly Effective 65%	$	17,745.00	6 $	2,957.50
Effective 35%	$	9,555.00	13 $	735.00
Ineffective 0%	$	-		
Base Pool Education Incentive 5%	$	19,500.00		
Highly Effective 65%	$	12,675.00	6 $	2,112.50
Effective 35%	$	6,825.00	13 $	525.00
Ineffective 0%	$	-		
Enrollment Incentive 10%	$	39,000.00		
Highly Effective 65%	$	25,350.00	6 $	4,225.00
Effective 35%	$	13,650.00	13 $	1,050.00
Ineffective 0%	$	-		
Support Staff Job Performance Incentive 4%	$	15,600.00		
Highly Effective 65%	$	10,140.00	8 $	1,267.50
Effective 35%	$	5,460.00	14 $	390.00
Ineffective 0%	$	-		

The table is continued on the next page.

CHARLES L. MOORE CPA

Example of Compensation

			Number of individuals who qualify	Total Compensation per individual
Base Student	$	210.00		
New Blend student count	$	310.00		
Net New Students	$	100.00		
State Aide amount	$	7,800.00		
Total New State Aide	$	780,000.00		
Teacher Education Incentive 7%	$	54,600.00		
Highly Effective 65%	$	35,490.00	6	$ 5,915.00
Effective 35%	$	19,110.00	13	$ 1,470.00
Ineffective 0%	$	-		
Base Pool Education Incentive 5%	$	39,000.00		
Highly Effective 65%	$	25,350.00	6	$ 4,225.00
Effective 35%	$	13,650.00	13	$ 1,050.00
Ineffective 0%	$	-		
Enrollment Incentive 10%	$	78,000.00		
Highly Effective 65%	$	50,700.00	6	$ 8,450.00
Effective 35%	$	27,300.00	13	$ 2,100.00
Ineffective 0%	$	-		
Support Staff Job Performance Incentive 4%	$	31,200.00		
Highly Effective 65%	$	20,280.00	6	$ 3,380.00
Effective 35%	$	10,920.00	13	$ 840.00
Ineffective 0%	$	-		

CHAPTER SIX

Where to From Here?

So, THE QUESTION lingering on the minds of people concerned about the education of our young people is, of course, where do we go from here? We can go over Brown v. Board of Education and take any number of stances in defense of whether it worked as intended or not. The truth of the matter is that there are no results to support that Title I has proved to be anything more than another failed Tuskegee Experiment at the expense of our young people. Will we allow the failure to linger another sixty years? It remains to be determined how many lives have been shortchanged to the point of no return through this experiment with those already most vulnerable in our society.

The school-to-prison pipeline has proved to be a one-way ticket for thousands of Black children. From within that group, we lost potential doctors, lawyers, inventors, husbands, fathers, and pillars of the community, all because their fate was set out before them at such a young age. No direction was given to guide them along the right path, giving them hope and a future. It has been spoken loudly to them that they would never amount to anything productive. As one of my fraternity brothers from the greatest fraternity in the world Omega Psi Phi, Bernard Crawford, says so eloquently, "It is impossible to rise to low expectations." We have gotten comfortable with these children failing and being lost in the poverty trap.

Young Black boys are disproportionately treated harsher for the same infractions that White boys commit. They are expelled at a significantly higher rate. Special education classes are filled with predominantly Black children. Their opportunities are limited to activities that dim their view of a future their ancestors dreamed of that education could afford them. They are set up to believe that they could not possibly achieve in a system where they look around them and everyone failing is just like them, Black, poor, and confused. Confused because they have grandmothers and elderly relatives who still remember the glimpse of the dream and hold on to the residue of hope that Brown v. Board of Education promised Black and poor folks.

Did we create another pipeline to prison by eliminating options for students who did not choose to attend college? Did we make their truth or consequences a one-way path to the streets for a life of crime or a ball and chain of manual labor with a nonliving wage attached? Today's generation simply cannot see the dream. They see a system that works for everyone else.

As we can see from previous chapters, almost everybody that got out of the poverty trap did not leave a roadmap or directions to their promised land. The most successful people you know, including your teacher, counselor, principal, doctor, lawyer, and nurse, have all left the neighborhoods so the ones left behind are left with no examples but the images they see on television or at school. Is it any wonder why kids stay in the office? Is it their way of trying to get to know the people that look like them so they can start a relationship? It is because the neighborhoods are not reflective of opportunity, but of heartbreak?

What about the teachers?

The Black population is roughly 40% in urban and poor areas, but the percentage of Black/Brown teachers is only 17%. This greatly affects learning when a child rarely sees someone like them. Black teachers have a tendency to believe in the Black child a bit more than the White teacher. Often, the White teacher feels that it is a waste of time and resources to pour into a child who does not want to and probably will not graduate. Again, that is a generalization. There are many White teachers that pour their soul into these children, while some of their Black teachers just see them as a paycheck.

We find that teachers are getting disenfranchised and quitting the profession at an alarming rate. In some places, the career expectancy for a teacher is five years or even less. They either move up to an administrative position to avoid the day-to-day interaction with the children for higher pay, move away from the ranks of those who are likely to be blamed for the failing system, or choose a totally different career path. The low wages, the lack of freedom, and other hindrances to the teaching profession have caused even those who love teaching to seek other fields. Over 26,000 African American teachers have left the profession. Despite the fact that the teaching profession has experienced an increase over the years, Black teachers are disappearing from school systems.

With our program, teachers are empowered to make changes again. In my mother's time, the community was motivated to supplement the income of teachers in various ways, as they knew that the power to achieve our educational dream was in the teachers' hands. In essence, this program will be doing the same thing, giving power back to those who CAN make a difference.

I can sit here like many of the other people in the education field and point out the obvious: that urban schools are failing the students that attend them. I suspect that some people who choose to take exception to this conclusion will also take exception when I say that we can put a person on the moon and develop cars that can drive themselves, but we cannot teach poor students how to read and write.

Because citizens, by and large, believe this failure is an injustice, we the citizens, foundations, and wealthy individuals have focused over three trillion dollars' worth of funding into the K–12 education system looking for improvement. The more we pump funds into the project, the worse it gets, and the more disenfranchised the individuals get. It is a fact that money is in failure.

There are more jobs created from the failure of these urban and poor students than from their success. Given the fact that, by and large, the professional staff of these districts have abandoned the communities for the greener pastures of the suburbs, parents are ill-equipped to assist financially or academically to improve their children's or grandchildren's educational trajectory. Without changing that trajectory, parents believe we should just start building more prisons or teach gun control in urban schools so that children can protect themselves from the criminal element that preys on them on a daily basis. These appear to be extreme options, but we are in extreme times when over 51% of children in urban areas still cannot read or write at a proficient level to obtain adequate employment. This is leading these students to street occupations. Is that the American way? Is that separate but equal?

The question is, was Brown v. Board of Education successful for Black women? Yes, but for Black men, no. For Blacks, in general, the answer is no. Black women have increased their income, obtained financial independence, and moved through the ranks of government and Corporate America. They were provided income sources that gave the least educated among them the ability to stay at home and raise the children, without Black men.

We have explored a lot of ideas in this writing. With or without statistical data, our common-sense conclusion is that Blacks are worse off than when Brown v. Board of Education was enacted as legislation. I will say that overall, the Black community is the net loser, although there are some winners. The Black college-educated group has increased by 400%, and their overall wealth has increased. But the wealth of Blacks continues to trail that of our White counterparts by a wide margin. The biggest winner is the educated Black woman. Their ranks have swelled during the past sixty years. Their wealth and control have far exceeded that of women of other races. They are graduating from college at a rate of seven to one compared to their Black male counterparts. The legal wealth in the neighborhoods is centered in the hands of the females.

The illegal wealth or the real wealth of control continues to be in the hands of the Black males. Well, maybe, that was the way the system was designed. Transfer the leadership of the Black community to the Black females and children, putting the Black male at a disadvantage and creating a feeling worse than the rape of the toughest Black man on the plantation, just to show how powerless they were. Let us one up on that. We give you equal opportunities, but we favor the women and children and erode or eliminate the need for the Black man for any reason besides to mate. Then they provide and take away all the opportunities for forward mobility.

One of the biggest barriers to upward mobility is the need for the Black man to be a man to their loved ones beginning at an early age. Although being from the neighborhood, the biggest barrier for those who want to make a life for themselves was not to have a child. Remember, if you had a child, you were afforded almost free housing, food, and other governmental protections. For the Black man, it led to having to become part of the system and having to get a job and take care of his new responsibilities. Without adequate skills to provide for the family's needs at a higher level than the government could, he was almost forced into the way of crime. This afforded him the best opportunity that his mind could envision for himself. If you remember, the flight of educated Blacks from the neighborhood has all but eliminated the Black educated role model in the "'hood," as it is affectionately known.

There was a demand for mates for child production. As I look back on it, I did not have good hair. The good-looking guys with the great hair were the ones in demand. It was unthinkable. It was almost an early retirement because you get a young lady who provided the food and shelter, and you could go out and get an unskilled cash job. Life was good. I just wanted to paint a picture of what the 'hood is really like. For some, it is not so bad, in fact, for the "wolf" that has respect, it can be a great living. Did you think going down memory lane affected the outcome of the landmark Supreme Court decision on Brown v. Board of Education?

The biggest net loser was the Black community itself. Before the decision, there was a common enemy, the fictional "White man."

Our communities' real fight was the Black man against the White man. Black men always wanted their children to have the opportunities that the White men could afford for their children. Do not get me wrong; there were some strong Black women that fought next to and, in some cases, in front of the Black man. In this case, the real fight was for the Black man to provide the opportunity. Most, if not all, the lawyers on the Supreme Court were White and Black men. The clear leadership was that the Black males that led in business ownership were pastors or were in government, education, and civil rights groups.

Blacks fought to live and work with Whites—to share equal opportunities and have the chance for educated Blacks to integrate into White society. Well, for the most part, that has happened. Blacks are teachers and principals of majority White schools. Blacks have been accepted as far as becoming president of the United States. But what about the people that do not get the opportunities for upward mobility, which is still 80% of Blacks in America?

The authors of Brown v. Board of Education could not have ever imagined that the individuals who would become the leaders in the Black community would not live and work in the Black community or almost disassociate themselves with the Blacks stuck in the neighborhoods. It is unthinkable that the unity that previously existed, which created the opportunities that now are afforded to some Blacks, has not permeated social consciousness enough for successful Blacks to reach back and bring forward their brothers and sisters from the old neighborhood. The traditional leadership of the balanced community largely moved to the suburbs of America. The sense of community pride that once flowed through the veins of the Black community is now almost no longer in existence.

One thing that the Black community authors of integration of the White community had was such a strong desire to reach their goals that they forgot about the home base, the 'hood. Their former neighborhoods were the biggest losers, which is ultimately a net loss for the Black community as a whole. Black togetherness led to the real failure of the Brown v. Board of Education legislation, which is the deterioration of the Black neighborhood. People that walk and drive past those 'hoods with disdain in their hearts may not understand that it was a set of laws that afforded them the opportunities to escape, and a reversal of those laws could push them back to the 'hoods they have so much disdain for. With the constant erosion of the Civil Rights Act of 1964 legislation, who knows what could happen?

Another thing that was consistently overlooked by the Black authors of the landmark decision was the integration of the Black community for business opportunities. The Black business owner clearly has been a target in the integration. Remember that in the Black community, vocational education was not only a part of the Black educational experience but also a necessity because we needed Blacks that could construct homes, fix cars, and do plumbing and electrical work. The trades were necessary to keep things running because there were two separate communities that serviced each community, with some crossover, but each community was somewhat self-sufficient. Now Black communities are about 75% dependent on service providers from outside the communities.

The Black politician has a strong alliance with unionized labor but more in common with the suburban educated population that opts to contract services from people they are more familiar with through educational connections, as opposed to the color of their skin. Construction has been a mainstay of the Black community since slavery. That industry is all but watered down now because the schools have eliminated vocational education and have eroded the interest of young Blacks. This has all but eliminated the trades as an opportunity for young Blacks. It wasn't the White men holding us back; it was the Black and Brown men and women who held leadership positions in their schools.

The Black church used to be the centerpiece of the Black community in the 1950s. An estimated 75% of the local Black community members attended church. Now, that level is 20%. Church leaders have also opted to pastor flocks in the urban neighborhoods but have moved their families to the suburbs, whether they are college-educated or not. Black church attendance is at an all-time low, which is eroding the influence of the Black church. The Black civil rights organizations are a mirror image of the Black church, basically consisting of the older Black population who are holding onto outdated traditions.

As you can see, urban and poor neighborhoods are ripe for exploitation. The traditional gatekeepers have been educators or educated pastors, business people, and civil rights groups, which now have all but abandoned Blacks in these neighborhoods. This is the reason I conjecture that there is money in the failure of students. It has brought about Title I, Medicaid, Medicare, Section 8, and other programs that provide assistance to Blacks in urban and poor communities.

These assistance programs are for the uneducated Blacks that are faced with barriers caused by sex, drugs, and violence. It is interesting how violence is almost always Black-on-Black crime, yet Black suburban leadership is mostly silent on the problem and the exploitation of Black males.

We watch news programs that show Blacks in other countries being exploited, and we post to social media about how bad it is. Yet we have the same thing happening in cities right here in America. When a White police officer shoots an unarmed Black person, the media and Black leadership exploit the situation and enrage the Black communities that they no longer live in. In no way am I condoning these actions, but I want to bring to the forefront that seven Black or Brown children were killed four blocks apart, and there was no public outcry, marching, or media attention because there was no money in the story and the media's families were, for the most part, not affected. Why? Because the murderers were Black themselves.

School systems now bring in charter schools, that have invested in the Black community, and alternatives to traditional public schools that are almost exclusively led by Black outsiders. The White "do-gooders" provide an opportunity for poor Black students to have a choice in their education. As I stated earlier, the natural entry to the Black community is through church pastors, because they are the voices for the community. Black pastors were the first and largest benefactors of the charter school movement. They gave charter schools access to the communities and lowered the voices of opposition to them.

Over the years, through financial or academic missteps, public schools have taken a back seat, and the movement toward charter schools has matured. Now the choice for Black children is accepted. As the Black suburban educator continued to underperform and not provide the educational experience wanted by a largely Black community, the community chose charter schools. As a direct rebuke to the poor Blacks they oversaw, educational leadership had systemically taken away the things that were most important to Blacks, including athletics, music, and industrial arts, which guaranteed poor Blacks a life of poverty. Whether you are Black or White, could you ever imagine seeing a day when suburban schools completely dominated urban schools in major sports and talent shows?

There you have it. The aftermath of the Brown v. Board of Education legislation is that it enslaves Blacks without using chains and transfers the educational overseer duties to the educated Blacks, for a fee, or it wouldn't be America. The wealth that was generated far exceeded the fee paid to the Black overseers. You have to keep some healthy tension between Blacks and Whites. That is the ingredient that keeps the wealthy free but in power.

When you give Blacks these kinds of opportunities, you provide the fuel that maintains the hate that dominates America today. Let's now add the major ingredient. You introduce the slave (local police) patrol, which is largely White, uneducated, and feeling left behind, and give them weapons to oversee the educated and uneducated Blacks and use all the resources that are available, and you have a recipe for disaster.

The question is, how do we fix it? That is the easiest part of the equation. If we can put people on the moon and develop cars that drive by themselves, we can teach kids in poverty how to read and write. Keep in mind there will be crimes to continue for the police. Why do you think there is still opposition to legalizing drugs, yet alcohol causes more deaths than marijuana? Seventy-five percent of police forces' cases are related to drugs. If you eliminate the drug cases, you eliminate the police workload. Then the police can start looking at things like white-collar crime.

The solution is within the theme of this book, which is "there's money in failure." We have to simply change the theme to "there's money in success." The union's labor force in education has promoted the same fair wages for teachers and support staff. I stated earlier that unions get paid on head count, not on performance, so the quality of education is a platform, but it is not a qualification for a raise and promotion. The job is to fight for increased staff compensation, but they have won the concession that their members do not have to live within the school district boundaries in which they work.

Ironically, because of the inferior education within urban and poor districts, stakeholders and leaders have moved their families to suburban districts for better opportunities. They lack a connection to the districts and the people to whom they deliver education. We have tried everything, including stronger teacher evaluations, competitions, new educational tools, and challenges. The results for urban educational tools and challenges have been abysmally poor because the "money is in failure." Even the charter schools that we provided as an opportunity for poor and undereducated communities to have different options have mixed results.

Because of a shortage of educators and increased requirements due to stagnant pay, the quality of teachers and support staff is at a historical low point—so much so that they are coming up with alternative paths to becoming certified teachers. This is interesting because the reduction and teacher shortages have come to a critical state in the urban education environment where the experiential methods are tied to the Title I demand for research information gathering. There are programs offered where you can get certified within six months to a year in any educational discipline, so people who are underemployed and want a career change can now educate primarily poor "at-risk" children. What in the hell has the world come to?

For the good people that want to improve education, you have to start providing additional salary support for Title XIII, the federal and state grant for performance. You have to keep in mind that up to now, we have tried to give bonuses for education but the union has been crying for more funds for teachers in the classroom based on the new demand. Remember most of the people that are making the rules for these grants somewhat want success, but if it does not occur, the children were supposed to fail anyway, because their parents are so screwed up—a convenient excuse.

Title XIII funding will be made up of a set of national standards for improvement. There will be a pool of funds that will be administered by the states and paid directly to the school staff that are affected. The way to get around the union fight for giving bonuses is that it will be administrative income over and above the contracted wages. There will be a dollar amount, for example, $300, for each "at-risk" student; and it will be paid out to all professional and support staff at the school. If your school has an application process that limits access or if you have less than 45% free or reduced-cost lunch program students, you are prohibited from participating in the grant program. For a school that qualifies for the Title XIII performance grant, if you have 1,000 students at $300 each, you receive $300,000 in bonuses if your school meets the national standards. Those bonuses are then paid to the staff based on the schedule submitted in the school improvement plan. Now, if your school fails, that $300,000 will go back into the pool of funds and given to the schools that were successful.

I wholeheartedly believe that school choice should be continued and possibly expanded, with one major caveat. The profit or nonprofit management companies' fees should be based on academic performance. It's un-American that we put "for profit" companies in to improve academic performance with competition when they haven't provided the results that were promised and continue to charge high fees for the buildings and school management. We do not have to put on restrictions, but the only way you can get the maximum management fee is if you meet or exceed the schools' academic goals. These fees would be reduced to no more than 2–5% of revenue if you underperform. That will also include the fee for the buildings that you rent. Below is a performance model for superintendents, principals, teachers, and support staff.

Superintendent	$23,625.00	$33,750.00	$28,350.00	$40,500.00	$35,437.50	$50,625.00	$44,296.88	$63,281.25

	Effective 50% or less of Free and Reduced	Highly Effect 50% or less of Free and Reduced	Effective 50% - 75% or less of Free and Reduced	Highly Effectiv 50% - 75% or less of Free and Reduced	Effective 75%-90% or less of Free and Reduced	Highly Effectiv 75%-90% or less of Free and Reduced	Effective 90% or greater of Free and Reduced	Highly 90% or greater of Free and Reduced
Principal	$17,500.00	$25,000.00	$21,000.00	$30,000.00	$26,250.00	$37,500.00	$32,812.50	$46,875.00
	$ -	$ -	$ -	$ -	$ -	$ -		
Teacher	$11,375.00	$16,250.00	$13,650.00	$19,500.00	$17,062.50	$24,375.00	$21,328.13	$30,468.75
	$ -	$ -	$ -	$ -	$ -	$ -		
Support Staff	$3,981.25	$5,687.50	$4,777.50	$6,825.00	$5,971.88	$8,531.25	$7,464.84	$10,664.06

There you have it, a model that pays a bonus for performance. Title VIII provides a pool of administrative funds to provide a bonus pool for schools building that performance. We have tried everything to improve education, so why not get a bonus? Right now, the poorest and worst-performing schools get, for the most part, the least of the talent pool. It is an easy equation if I am a high-performing teacher, why would I want to teach in a low-performing school with all the oversight and headaches that come with that assignment? The answer is clear: MONEY.

We have to do two things that will drastically improve education. First, attract better and more competitive talent to the ranks. Second, improve the pay of educators in underperforming schools. It is the American way for those that take the most risk and the most difficult assignments and are successful that they get paid more. Currently, the risk-reward is not there. The only way to improve the performance of children that are behind is to pay more money to those that take on the challenge of becoming successful. We can solve this problem with a bonus pool that is high enough to attract talent.

In my model, the schools with the highest poverty rates would get the highest amount of bonuses. But is that the way this should happen, and is the easy and existing calculation based on free and reduced-cost lunch counts? As you can see with the example in the appendix, the possible bonus amount will be spread over the complete school building staff. We used the school buildings as the way to distribute the bonus because most of the data is by building. It also promotes completion.

The data is available within the Title I data. It separates the schools by need, based on the percentage of free and reduced-cost lunch students attending the schools. The pool of funding for schools would be limited to the allocation per building, to be divided up. If there are other buildings that do not meet their goal, their funds would be transferred to the successful schools.

The bonuses top out at $63,281 for a superintendent in a district or charter school with a 90%+ at-risk population: $48,875 for a principal of a successful building, $30,368.75 for a teacher, and $10,604 for support staff in the building. These figures would only hold for a building that has 90%+ free and reduced-cost lunch students. However, you also have to be graded as highly effective. This would put the money where there is success. You would also let the principals pick their staff if they are going to be held accountable. This will draw additional talent to the industry into cities where the most vulnerable citizens live, using all the funds that we throw away on the failure model. State laws will be enacted to change management fees of for-profit or nonprofit management companies to fees based on academic performance.

In *The Aftermath of Brown v. Board of Education*, it is clear that the majority of urban children are worse off academically, socially, and emotionally after the decision was enacted. The students have actually been abandoned by most of the upwardly mobile staff and stakeholders. We do not want them moving back; we just want them to provide the education that was the promise and the dream when the Brown v. Board of Education legislation was passed.

Now the approach has to be different because education has been commercialized and compensation has to follow. Therefore, a bonus program that drives success must replace the failure models that are currently being used. Charles L. Moore, Jr.'s solution is to change the expectation and compensation to a successful model.

All the funds we use that place the emphasis on financially rewarding failure are against how we build America. The educator that takes on the risk of working with a concentration of at-risk students should be paid more. The model I developed does that and will provide the results that we have been looking for. If we can put a person on the moon, we can teach poor children how to read and write. We just have to direct the funding in that direction.

C. L. Moore & Associates work history

My company is located in the heart of Lansing, Michigan's downtown business district and on the east side of Detroit. We are a minority-owned firm that specializes in accounting and operational compliance for companies of all sizes. We received the SBA 8(A) certification in May 2014. C. L. Moore & Associates principal, Charles L. Moore, CPA, and its staff and associates are all seasoned and experienced banking, finance, and accounting professionals who have a long tenure in accounting and compliance matters. Through my work with C. L. Moore & Associates, I have served in capacities ranging from chief financial officer to internal auditor for large and small businesses. The company history and career background of Charles L. Moore (managing partner) are detailed below:

History of the Firm

The firm of C. L. Moore & Associates has been in operation since 1990. It provides full-service accounting services to individuals, businesses, and educational institutions. The firm's unique experience is in providing leased chief financial officer (CFO) services. It handles the day-to-day activities of a company's operation, which includes cash management, cash flow analysis, payroll services, bank statement reconciliation, bill payments, accounts receivable, invoicing, and loan negotiations. Through the "lease a CFO" program, C. L. Moore & Associates has managed over 660 employees. In this capacity, the firm oversees Michigan Occupational Safety and Health Administration (MIOSHA) compliance and hiring practices, and it reviews employee health benefits.

Experience of the managing partner, Charles L. Moore

Mr. Moore was employed with the state of Michigan's Department of Commerce (Bank and Trust Division) as a senior examiner. In that capacity, he was in charge of audits of banks with assets in excess of $25 billion. His primary function was to conduct operational audits of institutions, which included a review of operational systems, internal controls, stability of earnings, liquidity, and capital adequacy. These reviews concluded with a detailed report of problems and a recommended plan of correction.

Additionally, C. L. Moore & Associates has expanded its skills by serving in the capacity of interim internal auditor for the Lansing Board of Water & Light from August 2006 to June 2007. The firm continues to perform audit services for the Lasing Board of Water and Light, which is a $280 million operation with an estimated capital budget of $100 million. The auditing service primarily consists of compliance reviews, reporting pertinent and substantial findings, and making recommendations to the Board of Commissioners.

Mr. Moore has also served as an internal auditor for the Lansing School District and was very instrumental in developing and overseeing district compliance with the school board's approved policies, investigative issues, and reporting on management information systems. He also planned and prepared audit programs, directed the performance of audits, submitted audit reports to the comptroller, audited financial reports, assisted external auditors, and made recommendations for improvement in internal control in the accounting system. It should be noted that during his tenure, Mr. Moore assisted the chief financial officer and Board Finance Committee with improving the district's bottom line from $1,700,000 in 1995 to $32,000,000 in 1998.

C. L. Moore & Associates' relevant experience

• *Purchasing audits*

Reviewed bid documentation, adhered to established policies and procedures dictating purchasing, and reviewed approval processes

• *Departmental audits*

Reviewed operational efforts of departments relative to personnel, supplies, and activities to determine the appropriate budget alignments; reported transaction activities that occurred outside the budget approval process; and made recommendations to improve operational efficiencies up to and including the elimination of specific programs and FTEs

After completing the operational departmental audits referenced above and applying the recommendations that surfaced from the audit and budget reviews, the Lansing School District reversed seven years of operational losses. Notably, the trend of financial losses discontinued, and positive financial results occurred. The district's equity position ballooned to $34 million on $160 million in revenue. By contrast, the district's equity position at the beginning of the audit process was only $3.5 million on $160 million. These successes were not limited to the district's Internal Audit Department, but were a combined effort of Internal Audit, the Controller's Office, and the Superintendent's Office. The predominant footwork, however, was performed by Mr. Moore's office—Internal Audit.

• *Insurance and risk management audits*

C. L. Moore & Associates reviewed processes and procedures to ensure the appropriateness for risk tolerances based on industry trends and past history and accessed reserves and overall insurance coverage for institutional operations. The team reviewed the hospital's compliance with Medicaid and Medicare and its billing procedures. This provided management assurance that they were properly billing and in compliance with applicable Medicaid and Medicare policies and procedures.

- *Capital adequacy*

As a senior bank examiner, Mr. Moore reviewed the capital adequacy of financial institutions to ensure the availability of capital reserves in compliance with regulations.

- *Asset quality*

C. L. Moore & Associates reviewed asset quality of financial institutions, which included loans made to individuals; reviewed policy and practice for the adherence to industrial standards; and reviewed hard assets including buildings and real property, automobiles, and other tangible and intangibles listed on institution's balance sheets for the quality of these assets.

My background as a CPA and a bank regulator gives me the unique skills to assist special loan departments in working with problem credits. These skills can be used in situations where there is a forbearance agreement and monthly or quarterly monitoring is a requirement. It is my opinion that this would be a win-win for all parties.

- *Bank loan loss reserve*

C. L. Moore & Associates assessed reserve accounts for adequacy. This includes reviews of potential risk as compared to current reserve funding.

- *Human resource department audits*

Reviewed institutions' hiring, discipline, and vacation/annual leave policies; reviewed continuing education policies; reviewed benefits packages including health, dental, vision, and workman's compensation policies; reported on employee trends regarding absentee-ism; and made recommendations to reverse negative trends

- *Pension reviews*

C. L. Moore & Associates reviewed pension policies and proce-dures to assess the adequacy of investment returns and participated in the due diligence and RFP process of selecting fund managers to handle pension funds to ensure the maximization of investment returns while maintaining the quality of those investments. The higher level of returns that are available to the funds reduces the amount of contributions necessary for the company to meet actuarial projections, therefore improving the company's bottom line.

- *Bond sinking funds reviews*

Reviewed accounts for arbitrage, the distribution and manage-ment of funds, and the adherence to bond documents, policies, and procedures

- *Treasury services reviews*

Reviews include cash management assessments, long- and short-term investment reviews, and credit card processing services reviews. C. L. Moore & Associates developed recommendations for improvements to ensure adequate liquidity and to maximize invest-ment dollars while limiting credit exposure and assessed liquidity position and developed strategies to ensure the day-to-day availabil-ity of cash resources as well as long-term funding needs.

- *Cash management experience*

C. L. Moore & Associates provided day-to-day cash manage-ment for four institutions. This includes matching payables to cash receipts and utilizing lines of credits and other cash obligations for effective and efficient operations; negotiating and purchasing capital assets, buildings, buses, and construction loans for institutions; and managing the distribution of these funds and assets.

- *Construction management*

    C. L. Moore & Associates managed construction projects to ensure that all appropriate work is complete before draw requests are granted; attended construction meetings with engineers, architects, and crew leaders as the management's representative; and monitored project's progress for potential cost overruns and deadline deficiencies.

    C. L. Moore & Associates, as part of the Internal Audit Department at Lansing Board Water and Light, reviewed and performed a compliance audit on the construction project to build a $184 million cogeneration plant that was completed in July 2013. *Of note: the project was completed on time and on budget.*

- *Asset management*

    C. L. Moore & Associates assessed impaired assets; made recommendations to management on the disposition and distribution of assets; monitored the operation's compliance with applicable laws; and established accounting procedures relative to reported assets.

- *Forecasts and projections*

    Develop forecast and projection models on various segments of clients' business operations. This is done to assist management in developing decision-making policies relative to purchasing and organization staffing.

- *Information systems management*

    C. L. Moore & Associates reviewed established management information systems to ensure higher-level management receives appropriate information for informed decision-making.

I certainly hope this detailed background of C. L. Moore & Associates, its managing partner Charles L. Moore, and other staff is sufficient to articulate our experiences and expertise.

I am available to meet with you or your staff at your convenience to answer any additional questions. I look forward to hearing from you soon.

C. L. Moore & Associates
Charles L. Moore, CPA
Partner

STATISTICS IN AMERICA

Racial Diversity in American Schools

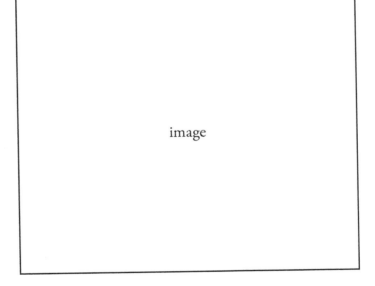

Incarceration rates

ACCORDING TO THE US Bureau of Justice Statistics (BJS) in 2013, Black males accounted for 37% of the total male prison population, White males 32%, and Hispanic males 22%. White females comprised 49% of the prison population in comparison to Black females who accounted for 22% of the female population.

Growth of the NAACP

The National Association for the Advancement of Colored People (NAACP) was founded in 1909 as a biracial endeavor to advance justice for African Americans.

BIBLIOGRAPHY

Fairbank, Greg. "The Problem with Urban Students? Their Teachers Leaving." *TEDx Wells Street ED*, November 13, 2013.

ABOUT THE AUTHOR

CHARLES L. MOORE is the owner of C. L. Moore & Associates, a certified public accounting firm in downtown Lansing, Michigan. C. L. Moore & Associates, founded in 1991, is one of the few minority-owned accounting firms in Michigan outside the Detroit area.

Having a background in politics, finance, and education, Charles L. Moore has dedicated his career to urban economic improvement and development. His company's lifetime work has been in pursuit of these ideals. He has worked as a CFO or internal auditor in public and charter schools primarily in urban settings. He has developed models that improved the financial stability of those urban schools that suffer from the high cost of educating poor children. He has poured his experience in these schools coupled with his own urban upbringing to author this book.

As a chairman of the Michigan Minority Supplier Development Council's Minority Business Enterprise Input Committee that helps the firms that provide professional service, leased employees, and insurance other than health insurance. He is also a board member of the Michigan State Board of Accountancy. Charles L. Moore, a native of Fort Wayne, Indiana, found his passion and dedication for economic development through his experiences in his hometown and seeing his community members struggle to provide for themselves and their families.

He has been married for eleven years and has three children who give him hope for the future of the state of Michigan, as well as the United States.

CPSIA information can be obtained
at www.ICGtesting.com
Printed in the USA
LVHW090508310721
694023LV00003B/614

9 781662 431456